CORRECT

EXPOSURE

In Photography

By

WILLARD D. MORGAN

and

HENRY M. LESTER

MORGAN & LESTER · *Publishers*

NEW YORK, N. Y.

CONTENTS

Contents

INTRODUCTION

The Photoelectric Exposure Meter has become a necessary tool to all photographers whether they are professionals engaged in photography for their livelihood or amateurs interested only in snapshots. The Exposure Meter can do many things for both if its uses are understood. The purpose of this book is to explain these uses.

The Exposure Meter is not a cure-all for all photographic ills. It will not make a master photographer over night. In itself it cannot be the means of attaining the ultimate in results, either in the art or technique of photography. But used intelligently it can be a valuable tool contributing much to the success of the photographer.

1. While incident illumination lights the subject, a photograph is made with reflected light or brightness.

2. Pictures like this are possible only by exposing the film correctly. Photo of Gale Storm by **Earl Theisen**.

Correct Exposure • The First
Necessity to Good Photography

LIGHT is the necessary tool of all photographers. They must use it to create their pictures . . . sunlight, skylight, arc lamps, tungsten bulbs or flash lamps. Light, irrespective of its source, is the brush which paints all photographs. Hence, of major importance to all photographers is the intensity of illumination present in the scene to be recorded on film and paper. For at all times approximately the same total amount should fall on the film if the negative is to show detail in the darkest shadows and brightest highlights—the exposure of the film to light must be correct if the photograph is to be successful.

The problem of correct exposure is perhaps the most important of all problems met by the photographer. This problem is difficult because of the necessity of judging light intensity, and important because it is the first step in the photographic process. If the exposure is incorrect, the photograph will be irrevocably lost.

Let us see what happens when the shutter clicks—or better, trace the path of light from its source to the sensitized film. Outdoors, the light source is usually the sun; its rays fall on the surface of the earth and illuminate it. The surface in turn reflects the light, and this reflected light is known as BRIGHTNESS. This light, this brightness, is effectively brought to a point by the camera lens, after which it spreads out again to form an image or flat miniature of the scene. Between the lens elements there is what might be termed a "quantity lock," a device for controlling the length of *time* the light falls on the film (the shutter) and one for controlling the amount of *light* falling on the film (the diaphragm or lens opening). Hence the controls of exposure are: the shutter to control the duration and the diaphragm, marked in f/ stops, to control the amount of light.

Light Intensity

A simple definition of correct exposure could be merely the proper quantity of light falling on the sensitized film for the *proper length* of time. If the photographer made his photographs under exactly the same conditions at all times, there would be no problem about correct exposure. By trial and error the correct combination of shutter speed and f/ stop could be arrived at, the camera set and henceforth this exposure would of necessity be exactly right. Fortunately for the sake of variety and life in the art, this is not the case.

The sun is used by amateur and professional photographers for more pictures than any other light source. Yet the intensity of sunlight varies from one day to another, from one scene to another, from one period of the day to another. These facts are well known even to the layman, but they are of the utmost importance to the photographer. *Here is the first factor influencing exposure, the light source and its variations, whether the source be the sun, a photoflood or a spotlight.*

The second factor is the scene itself. It is obvious that some objects reflect more light than others. Some scenes are dark because of their surface character while others are bright for the same reason. More light is reflected from a bright beach than a grassy lawn even though the same amount of sunlight falls on both. The same exposure would not be given to both scenes, even though the light source were the same in each case.

The distance of the light source from the subject or scene is the third factor influencing exposure. For instance, a portrait light is less intense the farther away it is from the subject.

The factors all concern themselves with *light intensity!*

1. Intensity of source.
2. Intensity of reflected light as controlled by the subject.
3. Intensity of light as influenced by distance.

(In passing it would be wise to point out that exposure is *not* dependent upon nor influenced by the distance of the camera from the scene except when the distance is very small as in close-ups. The well-known law of inverse squares is not significant to this application) .*

* The intensity of illumination from a point source of light varies inversely as the square of the distance from that source to the surface upon which it falls. See page 105.

Since all the factors controlling exposure concern themselves ultimately with the intensity of light *reflected* from the scene, the problem of correct exposure can be solved easily by measuring this reflected light. This is not a particularly new idea. Photography as we know it today grew out of the efforts of two men, Hurter and Driffield. They recognized that the problem of correct exposure could be and should be solved by light measurements. But at that time there was no simple way of measuring light. They tried to do this by using a sensitized paper, exposing it until it had darkened to match a standard tone, the time necessary to do so being the criterion of the light intensity. Their instrument is now known as an actinometer. Outside of its inherent errors, it measured only incident illumination, which disregarded the influence of the scene surface—a serious omission.

Various men coming after Hurter and Driffield tried to solve the problem with as many different devices. Notable among these devices was the extinction type of exposure meter. The extinction meter took many forms, the best known perhaps being the step wedge type. Here a strip of film graduated in steps of density was used. The photographer looked through this wedge and the number of the step which was just barely visible was considered the light value. The principle of the extinction meter was good, but the sensitive element, the eye, was bad. The human eye can judge light intensities only with difficulty. As a protective measure the iris of the eye closes rapidly upon exposure to bright light, and opens very slowly when that light is removed. Since the eye automatically compensates for changing light intensity, naturally it cannot measure the absolute value of any light intensity.

Recently a noted professional photographer remarked that the photographic industry owed an everlasting vote of thanks to the inventor of the batteryless photoelectric cell. For it was this photoelectric cell that paved the way to an easy solution to a vexing and troublesome problem. With the photoelectric cell, the active imagination of a talented electrical engineer with photography as a hobby, and the application of science to a scientific problem, came the batteryless photoelectric exposure meter.

9

What Is an Exposure Meter?

The photoelectric exposure meter overcame all the short-comings of former attempts at solving the problem but one—it still would not think. Thus, it is still necessary for the photographer to use his brain in company with his meter if he would obtain the optimum results.

Before learning how to use an exposure meter, it may be of interest to know what a meter is and of what the instrument is made. Briefly, a meter is made up of three parts which are:

1. The light measuring element: the photoelectric cell.
2. An electrical instrument to measure current, which is proportional to light intensity.
3. A device to correlate light measurements, film speed and camera settings: the exposure guide dial.

The photoelectric cell is a strangely fashioned affair which changes light energy to electrical energy. The electric current produced is proportional to the intensity of light falling on it. Connected to the cell is the electrical instrument which measures this current, but instead of reading in electrical values, the instrument indicates light values directly. So here is a real light meter, a device to measure the factors of exposure.

To correlate the scene light value to the controls of exposure, the camera settings, an exposure guide dial is provided. In different models, the exposure guide dials take different forms, but their primary function is the same—to correlate the *factors* of exposure with the *controls* of exposure.

Not part of an exposure meter but essential to its use is the film rating system, an accurate, impartial and uniform method of rating the emulsion speeds of films so that the exposure meter can be adjusted to any type of emulsion. At this moment, the mechanics of rating films need be of no concern. But of its necessity there is no doubt. The system chosen for Weston exposure meters was one built from scratch and based on the characteristic H & D curve of the film. Later we will investigate the actual workings of the method for rating film.

The necessary parts of an exposure meter have been put together to solve the problem stated far back, to measure the light reflected from the scene. This was an old, accepted and sound premise. But the inventor of the modern exposure meter realized

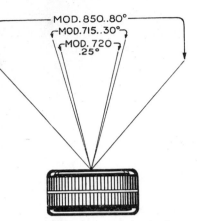

3. The controls of exposure are the f/ stop and the shutter speed; the former affecting the amount of light, the latter the time the light acts on the film.

4. *The acceptance angles* of three Weston Exposure Meters. The narrower the angle, the more directional is the meter.

that it was not enough to measure reflected light; it was necessary to measure only the part of the reflected light that would be seen by the camera lens. In other words the meter had to be selective, just as the camera lens is selective. Usually the camera views a scene through an angle of from 30° to 60°; this angle is known as the acceptance angle of the camera.

To make the meter selective, or approximate the viewing angle of the camera, a restrictive baffle is used in front of the photoelectric cell. In general, the more nearly the acceptance angle equals that of the principal part of the scene, the more accurate the exposure will be. Certainly it is obvious that the smaller the angle, the more directional the meter will be.

The acceptance angle of an exposure meter controls the area of the scene the meter will view. An exposure meter is much like a camera; it is equipped with a kind of lens and diaphragm, a sensitized surface (the cell) and it is affected by the reflected light from the scene. To draw another analogy the meter is really a flashlight in reverse. The flashlight sends out a cone of light having its apex at the bulb and casts a circle of light on whatever surface at which it is pointed. The meter receives light from a circular area of whatever surface at which it is pointed, the apex of the cone being the cell surface. The wider the ac-

11

ceptance angle, the wider will be the circle from which the meter will receive light, and hence the less directional it will be.

It might be interesting to compare acceptance angles. The accompanying diagram will show graphically the angles of view of a number of Weston instruments.

A good general rule for the selection of an exposure meter in regard to acceptance angle is to reject any instrument having an angle over 90°. Those with larger angles will not lend themselves to the approved methods of use described in this book nor will their accuracy be sufficient for anything but run-of-the-mill black and white snapshots.

Summary

1. The factors which influence exposure are all concerned with the light reflected from the scene.
2. For accurate control of exposure this reflected light must be measured by an instrument independent of the human eye. The photoelectric type of meter meets this need.
3. This exposure meter must be used intelligently—it won't think by itself.

Exposure Experiments

1. Inspect five or six different types of scenes such as an outdoor portrait, an interior, landscape, scene in deep shadow and a brightly illuminated street scene.
2. Using your own judgment, determine the camera setting for a specific film (one having a speed of 50 Weston for example).
3. Then use your exposure meter to determine the camera settings—notice the great difference.

Choosing The Meter

Every photographer recognizes the need for a meter, but —which meter? An exposure meter should be suited to the photographer's own particular needs, for some meters are better or more convenient for some purposes than for others.

A short discussion on various models of exposure meters, their salient features and their particular recommendations will help in making a choice. Most photoelectric exposure meters essentially do the same thing, they measure reflected light. The difference among the instruments is one chiefly of calibration and calculator design—and, of course, the price mark. As with practically everything else in the world, a meter's worth is usually indicated by the price charged for it.

The characteristics one should look for in an exposure meter are few, but important. First of all, the instrument should have sufficient range to accommodate any light condition which the user might meet. By range is meant the highest reading the meter will indicate and the lowest. The higher the top mark and the lower the low reading, the greater the range. The photographer who expects to expose a quantity of film to scenes very dimly lighted would naturally need the most sensitive meter available—sensitive in terms of its lowest scale reading. On the other hand, the amateur who makes outdoor pictures exclusively, or interiors only when there is an abundance of light, would not need extreme sensitivity. He could buy a less sensitive meter and save the difference.

A man interested solely in black and white snapshots may not need the accuracy for color of a Master meter. The less expensive Junior meter will meet all his needs. The man interested only in snapshots of his many and varied experiences might

5. *The Model 715 Master*—the universal instrument for every photographer. Particularly needed by the advanced amateur and professional.

not have occasion to use the control possible with a Universal type of meter.

The photographer interested only in ciné photography will want an instrument particularly designed for ciné work, while he who has both a ciné and still camera will want, if possible, a meter for both.

Here are the specifications of the four Weston Exposure Meters together with a few recommendations concerning them.

Weston Master Universal—Model 715

This is the most accurate and sensitive exposure meter available. It is equipped with a scene classification dial which enables the photographer to control his exposures and obtain very uniform results. The limits of film ranges for both black and white and color are indicated. These limiting marks are most helpful, for with them the amateur can expose for specific objects and control the ultimate over-all density of his negatives.

For an increased range, the meter is equipped with sliding scales, one 0-50 and the other 0-1600. In effect this means two meters in one. These scales shift automatically when an external baffle is opened or closed, so that there is no chance for confusion.

The Model 715 is the meter most popular with both amateur and professional photographers. The specifications listed

14

below will enable you to compare this instrument with other models.

Accuracy:	⅙ f-stop.
Sensitivity:	First readable deflection .2 candle per sq. ft.
Scale Length:	1.32 inches.
Range:	Maximum reading, 1600 candle. Minimum reading .2 candle. Ratio: 8000.
Acceptance Angle:	30° high scale, 80° low scale.
Calibration:	Candles per sq. ft. (A measure of reflected light).

The Master is recommended for all those who are really serious about photography. It is particularly recommended for the color photographer or those using color film in their cameras. This instrument, as the name Universal implies, can be used with all kinds of cameras, both still and ciné.

Weston Master Ciné – Model 720

This meter is very similar to the Model 715 but is calibrated for ease of use with motion picture cameras. The same cell and the same type of electrical instrument is used in the two meters, but the Ciné Master is not as sensitive. Because motion pictures are a series of instantaneous exposures, the camera ob-

6. *The Model 720 Master*—the exposure meter for the advanced amateur and professional cinematographer.

viously cannot be operated for long-time exposures. Therefore the sensitivity of a meter for cinematography can be sacrificed somewhat for a narrower acceptance angle. While high speed movie films have opened up a large field of possibilities for comparatively dark scenes and interiors, nevertheless the sensitivity of this meter is more than enough for all these possibilities. An interesting thing about these Master meters is the fact that their cells are hermetically sealed as a protection against excessive moisture. The Ciné Master also has two shifting scales.

Specifications:

Accuracy:	$\frac{1}{6}$ f-stop.
Sensitivity:	First readable deflection representing 0.8 candle per sq. ft.
Scale Length:	1.51 inches.
Range:	Maximum reading represents 3600 candles. Minimum reading represents .8 candle. Ratio: 4500.
Acceptance Angle:	25° high scale, 60° low scale.
Calibration:	Arbitrary reflected light values.

This meter is recommended for all those seriously interested in cinematography. Most movie makers use more color than black and white these days and for them this meter should be ideal because of its narrow selective angle and its accuracy. While it can be used for still photography if necessary, it is not as convenient for that purpose. If you intend doing both kinds of work, the Universal meter would be better.

Weston Junior Universal—Model 850

This meter was designed so that expensive features not needed by the snapshooter could be eliminated. Hence one need not pay for material which he neither will use or need. The Junior is very easy to use, and many own it for that reason.

Specifications:

Accuracy:	$\frac{1}{2}$ f-stop.
Sensitivity:	First readable deflection representing 0.8 candle per sq. ft.

7. *The Model 850 Junior*—the universal instrument for the occasional picture taker or beginner.

8. *The Model 850 Junior Cine*—the exposure meter for the occasional or beginner movie maker.

Scale Length: 1.33 inches.

Range: Maximum reading represents 2300 candles. Minimum reading represents 1.3 candles. Ratio: 1 = .1800.

Acceptance Angle: 80°.

Calibration: Arbitrary reflected light values.

The Junior is particularly recommended for the photographer who does not wish to concern himself with the finer points of photography. Beginners and occasional picture takers will probably prefer the Junior to the Master meters. The sensitivity is considerably less than in the more expensive instruments, hence it cannot be used where the light is very poor. It is satisfactory for all types of outdoor scenes and many well-lighted interior ones. It can be used for both ciné and still cameras.

Weston Junior Ciné—Model 850

This meter occupies the same position with relation to the Junior Universal as the Model 720 does to the Master Universal. The meter is practically direct reading and is very simple in operation. Where space is at a premium, the Junior may fit in where the larger ones do not. Specifications:

Accuracy: ½ f-stop.
Sensitivity: First readable deflection 6 candles per sq. ft.
Scale Length: 1.33 inches.
Range: Maximum reading represents 1800 candles. Minimum reading represents 6 candles. Ratio: 300.
Acceptance Angle: 80°.
Calibration: Arbitrary reflected light values.

Beginners and occasional movie makers will find this meter quite sufficient for their needs. It is not recommended for still photography. The individual interested in both fields of photography would be wise in obtaining a Universal meter rather than the Ciné model, since the latter is not very sensitive and hence cannot be used under extremely adverse light conditions indoors, though it is perfectly satisfactory for outdoor use.

Here, then, are the listings of the important specifications of the popular and universally accepted Weston meters. Choose the one for your needs. But let that choice be dictated by what you will really need.

In the past the Universal Model (Model 650) has been the most popular meter in the Weston line and now the greatly improved Master Universal (Model 715) is, by far, the leader in the photographers' preference. Since these Universal meters are owned ten to one over other types, the major portion of this book will be confined largely to them.

Using The Meters · · ·

The Camera Position

THERE isn't anything particularly difficult in photography, for there wouldn't be twenty million people in this country enjoying the hobby if there were. There isn't anything difficult in the use of exposure meters either. So let's not make it too hard for ourselves, and learn a simple and reasonably accurate method of using a photoelectric exposure meter.

The simplest and quickest method of using a meter is from the camera position; that is, the place where the camera is located. It doesn't matter whether the camera is at the top of a sky-scraper or five feet from the subject, the camera position reading will yield a well exposed negative.

Alice, of the delightful Alice in Wonderland, was once told that the proper thing to do was to "start at the beginning and keep on going until you come to the end—then stop!" That advice is excellent. The beginning is the way to hold a meter. The illustration shows better than words how a meter should be held. There is no rule against holding a meter any way one chooses, but this seems to be the most convenient. Remember that although the photoelectric cell is truly a magical device, it cannot see through fingers, so keep the fingers from in front of the cell. Some feel that the meter should be shielded by the fingers. Usually this is not necessary, but wherever a lens hood would be used on a camera, the cell of the meter could be hand shielded.

The next step is aiming the meter. First let us visualize a scene composed of two parts, the ground and the sky. If the ground is correctly exposed, the sky will probably be overexposed. And if the exposure for the sky is correct, the darker portions of the ground will be underexposed. For light from the sky is more actinic than that reflected from the ground; an exposure meter's sensitivity is very similar to the film sensitivity, and naturally the light to which a photographic film is most sensitive will affect an exposure meter in the same way.

Hence in using a meter the photographer will not concern himself with the sky, but will measure the light reflected only from the ground.

Considering the horizon line in the scene as one spot and the photographer's feet as another, the exposure meter should be aimed downward, at a point halfway between. This will eliminate undue effect of the sky, and the meter will measure only the light from the foreground. If the tone of the sky is to be controlled, it should be done by means of a filter, not by exposure. After aiming the meter, the light value for that scene can be read on the dial. And thus the fundamental purpose of the meter is achieved—to measure the light reflected from the scene.

In aiming the meter, the photographer should remember what the meter sees: a circular area, the base of a cone of light, the apex of which is at the cell surface of the instrument. This circle should be on the ground and not in the sky. Probably 95% of exposure errors come from failure to tip the meter downward.

9, 10. (Left) *Holding the exposure meter.* Any way would do as long as the fingers do not obstruct the view of the cell, but here's a convenient method. (Right) Set the normal arrow to the light value indicated by the meter, and choose a camera setting. In this case it was f/11 at 1/50 of a second.

11. A simple landscape for which correct exposure is obtained through the use of the camera position method. Stephen H. Willard photo.

After reading off the light value, the second part of the meter is used—the exposure guide dial which translates light values into camera settings. The emulsion rating of the film in use should first be set in the emulsion rating window. Then the large dial arrow index of the Master Universal type of meter should be set to the same number as the measured light value.

At the bottom of the exposure guide dial will be found a series of f stop and shutter speed combinations. After setting the dial, any of these combinations will yield a correct exposure. The choice of a combination will depend entirely upon what the picture is. If there is action in the scene, a fast shutter speed will be necessary, and hence the shutter speed will determine the f-stop. For example, a choice of from 1/250 of a second at f/4.5 to ⅕ of a second at f/32 might be indicated. If there is fast action, the former combination should be chosen. On the other hand, if there is no action in the scene, then a small stop would be desirable for maximum depth of field. In that case, the

21

f-stop would determine the shutter speed. For the conditions mentioned above, the exposure chosen for a scene with no motion would probably be f/32 at ⅕ of a second.

The choice of the actual exposure settings deserves more than a mere passing mention. Too many amateurs feel that the rapidity of the shutter speed is the entity to solve all their problems. They are enchanted by fast lenses, fast films, fast shutters, and glowing promises of excellence through their use. When there is fast action in the scene to be photographed, of course there is little choice—a rapid shutter speed, fast film and wide f-stop are necessary. But few scenes require all that speed. By stopping down the lens, a greater over-all sharpness can be achieved.

Photography is one art where objects can be reproduced in all the sharpness seen by a normal pair of human eyes. Use small stops where possible. Without a tripod, no slower shutter speed than ⅟₅₀ of a second should be attempted unless the photographer has extraordinarily steady nerves. Naturally, a tripod is a very worth-while investment. Watch a professional photographer; when possible he uses a tripod on practically every picture.

A great majority of the scenes met by the average photographer can be successfully exposed by setting the normal arrow opposite the light value shown by the meter. Sometimes, however, scenes which are exceptionally flat are met. When there is little inherent contrast in the scene itself and when this scene is flatly illuminated, a shorter exposure is desirable. Such scenes

12. *For distant views,* point the meter downward to avoid measurement of the sky, which would give incorrect exposure for the darker foreground and land areas.

13. Good detail in the shadow portions of this picture by F. S. Lincoln proves that the photographer can choose the exposure by using his meter correctly.

23

Flat vs. Contrasty Scenes

will be found on deserts, beaches, in the winter when snow is on the ground and where the subjects of interest are at a great distance from the camera—commonly classified as distant views. For these flat scenes the shorter exposure can be very conveniently arrived at by using the "A" position on the exposure guide dial set opposite the light reading instead of the "normal" arrow.

Good photographic technique indicates a longer development than normal for negatives exposed to flat scenes. By reducing the exposure, the over-all density of the negatives is kept printable without excessive printing times, and the photographer's negatives can be kept more nearly uniform.

The opposite of the flat scene is, of course, the excessively contrasty scene. A longer exposure than normal is desirable for the contrasty scene and this can most conveniently be achieved by using the "C" position on the exposure guide dial. After taking the reading from an excessively contrasty scene, the "C" position should be set opposite the light value shown by the meter, instead of the "normal" arrow.

A longer development time than normal would increase the over-all density, and as mentioned above this over-all density is kept to normality by a shorter exposure through the use of the "A" position. The contrasty scene is just the reverse of

14, 15. The wrong and right way of taking a camera position reading. In left photo the meter measures too much sky, which will lead to under-exposure. Tip the meter downward as in the picture at the right.

24

16. A scene like this, having more contrast than is considered normal, is known as a "long range" scene. The "C" position should be used instead of the normal arrow.

the flat scene. To achieve good printability of a negative of a contrasty scene, the development should be considerably shorter than usual. But to compensate for the resultant lack of over-all negative density, the exposure is increased through the use of the 2X, or "C" position.

Thus it is apparent that through the use of the "A" and "C" position, more uniform negative density can be obtained. It should be pointed out, however, that if the photographer is in doubt, the normal arrow will give him correct exposure. The "A" and "C" positions will only enable him to have more uniform negatives.

With the Junior and Ciné types of meters the same technique of pointing and aiming the meter should be observed. But the "A" and "C" compensations cannot be made. These instruments are very easy to use, and the dial setting can be learned quickly from the instructions.

25

Summary

Summary

1. For camera position readings, the meter should be aimed at a point halfway between the horizon line and the photographer's feet.
2. Use the normal arrow for normal scenes, the "A" position for flat and the "C" position for contrasty ones.

Exposure Experiments

1. Choose a landscape, point the meter at the sky and make an exposure using the resultant settings.
2. Duplicate, but point the meter downward as recommended.
3. Notice the difference in the negatives. Only No. 2 will produce a good print.

17. Balancing the exposure to bring out some details in the shadow produces the plastic feeling of three dimensions and depth. **F. S. Lincoln** photo.

The Close-up Method

THIS section will be necessarily short, for simplicity does not require a lengthy explanation. The close-up method of using an exposure meter is just what the title suggests—the meter is held close to, or "close-up" to the subject being photographed so that average exposure will be given to that specific subject.

The close-up method should be used when there is one object in which the photographer is particularly interested surrounded by a background greatly different in brightness. For example, a person whose face is shaded might be standing in front of brilliantly lighted white concrete. The face of that person would be of particular interest; therefore, the photographer would expose specifically for the face. And he could most conveniently do this by taking a close-up reading.

The meter should be pointed directly at the subject and held the same distance away as the subject's smallest dimension. Perhaps the object might be 8 by 10 inches in size. The meter should be held about 8 inches away. Of course, this distance need not be exact—there is no need of measuring distances and dimensions. The average person can estimate distances well enough for this purpose. Incidentally, the meter can be held as close as the user wishes, but *not further away* than the object's *smallest* dimension.

What is desired is to measure only the surface area of the subject. Since an exposure meter measures light per unit area (*candles*—per *square foot*), it doesn't matter whether the meter views one square foot or ten, it will still indicate the light reflected per unit area. Therefore, the meter can be held 10 inches away from a 10 by 10 inch object as well as 10 feet away from a 10 by 10 foot object and the same light reading will be indicated, provided both are the same color and both are similarly illuminated.

After reading off the light value for the subject, the "normal" arrow of the universal type of meter should be set opposite that value on the exposure guide dial, and the exposure settings chosen.

With very wide angle meters, the distance the meter should be held away from an object would, of course, be less than that suggested. For the area covered or viewed by a meter depends upon this angle—the larger the angle, the greater coverage for a given distance. With meters other than Weston the rule mentioned cannot be used. For a given object, the reading of the meter will be the same, regardless of the distance from the meter to that object until the meter starts to view more than the area of the subject, then the reading will change. Hence, with wide angle meters, the user can easily determine when he is measuring only the surface in which he is interested, and when other objects are beginning to be picked up by his meter. For all Weston meters, the rule of the "same distance from, as the distance across" will be quite satisfactory.

18, 19. (Left) When taking a close-up reading, do not cast a shadow of the meter onto the subject. Here the girl is measuring a dark shadow rather than the bright rocks. (Right) Backlighted portraits also require a close-up reading. Take it from the face and set the normal arrow to the value obtained.

20. The close-up method is a good one for pictures of people at the beach. Hold the meter about eight inches from the face.

When taking a close-up reading, care should be taken not to cast a shadow of the meter onto the object being measured. For very small objects, it may be necessary to hold the meter at an angle to the direction from which the light is coming. With such an angular reading, it is easily possible to measure an object only a few inches across. The accompanying illustrations show how this can be done.

Some photographers, knowing of the inverse square law of light, have felt that a close-up reading would not be correct because, since light intensity decreases inversely as the square of the distance, the illumination of the subject would not be the same at the camera lens as at the position of the meter being held close to the subject. This, however is an erroneous deduction. See page 105—The Inverse Square Law.

The close-up method is simplicity itself, but let us visualize a few types of scenes where it would be useful. For example, a backlighted outdoor portrait might be the object of the photographer's lens. Here the face of the subject should have average normal exposure. This can be achieved by using the close-up method. Or the object of interest might be in dark shadow while the background would be brightly illuminated. Here again the close-up reading would be desirable—and vice versa.

For table-tops, or other single object photographs illuminated by artificial light, the close-up reading will yield an average normal exposure for good results.

Summary

1. Where one object in the scene is most important, a close-up reading will yield a normal exposure for that object.
2. To take a close-up reading, the meter should be held about the same distance from the object as that object's smallest dimension.

Exposure Experiments

1. Choose a scene where the principal object is small and dark situated in a large area of brightly illuminated surroundings (for example, a beach scene where the principal object is backlighted). Make an exposure using the meter from the camera position.
2. Duplicate, but use the close-up reading method.
3. Only No. 2 will produce a good reproduction of the principal object; it will probably be underexposed in No. 1.

The Brightness Range Method

THE photographer not interested in exposure control can get along quite nicely with the camera position and close-up methods of using an exposure meter. But the more particular man may wish to have more control over exposure.

The most precise control and the most accurate exposure can be achieved through the measurement of object brightnesses and exposing midway between the darkest and brightest objects in the scene.

Every scene is made up of objects reflecting different amounts of light—in other words, of objects having different brightnesses. In the scene shown on page 33, it can be seen that the tree with a light value of 25 is darker than the dress having a light value of 250. The dress in turn is darker than the young lady's face which has a light value of 400.

A good photographer tries to show all objects in the scene in the same light relationship as the original, and he will strive to hold both shadow detail and highlight modeling. To do this, the first step is naturally correct exposure for both the shadows and the highlights. He can be sure of this only by exposing for an object midway between the darkest shadow and the brightest highlight.

The brightness range method is easy. To do this take close-up readings of the various objects in the scene, then by setting the normal arrow on the exposure guide dial half-way between the lowest value and highest, expose for the middle object without actually measuring that object. In setting the arrow be sure that the darkest object light value on one side equals the same "blocks" away on the brightest light value side.

Advantages of Brightness Range Method

Remember, in taking the close-up reading, the meter should be held about the same distance away from the object being measured as that object's smallest dimension. Do not cast a shadow of the meter onto the object.

A typical scene might be composed of trees, grass, and other objects. A close-up reading will show that the darkest object will probably be the tree trunk and the brightest the sunlighted grass. If the tree has a value of 25, and the grass one of 200, the normal arrow would be set at 65. The photographer should not average the two extremes when using a universal meter. In the above example, an average value would be 112:5; yet when the normal arrow of the meter is centered between the two extremes it would show that the arrow was at 65.

There are a number of advantages to this method of using a meter. A technical one is that the exposure is centered on the characteristic H & D curve of the film material. In so doing, the best possible reproduction from an exposure viewpoint will be achieved. And that, of course, is what the photographer strives to do—obtain the best possible reproduction of the scene. He must remember, though, that exposure is not everything in photography. And to obtain accurate reproduction, the other steps in the process must also be correct. But if the exposure is not correct, no amount of manipulation in the succeeding steps can compensate for it.

Another advantage of the brightness range method is that by its use the full range of the film can be utilized. For very long range or contrasty scenes this is quite important. The average film range (black & white) is restricted to about 1 to 130. By this is meant that it will handle and correctly expose objects having brightness from 1 to 130, 2 to 260, 3 to 390 or any other multiple, but the ratio between the brightest and darkest objects both of which will be correctly exposed is limited to the figure of approximately 1 to 130. For short range, or flat scenes, great accuracy in exposure is not too necessary. The one-reading method of using the meter is quite sufficient. But where the range of the scene (ratio between the light values of the darkest and brightest object) approaches the range of the film, the necessary accuracy of exposure can be achieved only by the two-reading method.

32

21. Every scene is made up of objects reflecting different amounts of light. The exposure meter can quickly and accurately determine these light variations.

The brightness range method will work satisfactorily under all photographic conditions, and with it there is little or no chance for error. We heartily recommend it for any photographer past the snapshot stage.

Later on in this book you will find that through the use of brightness range measurements, development of the film can be controlled so that all negatives can be printed on the same grade of paper—another advantage of measuring the scene range and exposing accordingly.

With exposure meters calibrated in arbitrary light values such as the Weston Junior or Ciné meters, the technique of setting the exposure guide dial is a little different. With these meters, the close-up reading is taken the same as with the Universal types. But here the two values are *averaged,* and the average value used in setting the dial. For example, the brightest object might have a light value of 20 and the darkest, 8. The scene light value should then be considered to be 14, and the dial set accordingly.

Sometimes it will be found either impossible or inconvenient to take close-up readings. In that case, objects close at hand, similar to the actual objects in the scene, can be substituted. Suppose, for example, that the subject is a young lady, her face half in sunlight, half in shade, leaning against a dark tree trunk,

22. In this picture, the tree trunks are obviously the darkest objects and the sunlighted white building the brightest. It is often necessary and desirable to utilize the full range of the film. This can be done by using the brightness range method. F. S. Lincoln photo: St. George-Tucker House, Williamsburg, Va.

23, 24. (Left) A close-up reading of the tree trunks in this scene is being determined. (Right) The back of the hand can be substituted for a person's face. If the face is in sunlight, the hand should be in sunlight; if in shade, the hand should be in the shade.

the foreground being made up of grass. There is no necessity to take actual close-up reading. The grass at one's feet has the same composition as the grass in the scene. A nearby tree will be the same as the tree in the scene; even a substitute can be found for the young lady's face—the back of your hand, shaded to represent the shaded portion of the face, and held directly in sunlight for the sunlighted part.

Another example might be an island in a lake, the island being the principal object in the scene. Shadowed portions of the island could be measured by measuring shadows close to the camera. Sunlighted grass could be found close at hand to substitute for the grass in the distance. Sunlit or shadowed trees could also be found close at hand to be measured instead of those on the island. Thus for all objects in the distance, the photographer can find similar objects close to him which can be measured.

Of course, if the object in the scene is in direct sunlight, then the substituted object should be in direct sunlight. And if shadowed, the substituted object should be shadowed.

Summary

1. Close-up readings of the darkest and brightest objects in the scene.
2. Centering the exposure by balancing the normal arrow of the

exposure guide dial halfway between the two extremes thus
measured.

3. Substitution of convenient, nearby objects for those in the
scene which are either inaccessible or inconvenient to
measure.

Exposure Experiments

1. Choose a long-range (contrasty) landscape and make three
negatives using
   A. The camera position method.
   B. Close-up method (choose an object as the principal one).
   C. The brightness range method.
2. Develop and print. Note that the best exposure was obtained
by using the brightness range method.
3. Take a close-up reading from the back of your sunlighted
hand, and one from a friend's face, also sunlighted. Note that
the readings are practically the same. This shows the accuracy
of substituted readings.

Color Photography and

The Exposure Meter

THERE are few photographers who have not felt the thrill of making pictures in full color. All who have made color photographs have also found out that exposure for color must be very much more accurate than for black and white. As a matter of fact, an exposure measurement for color must be many times more accurate than for black and white for the same relative quality of results.

Now this sounds rather terrifying. But not at all; color is easy if the very important step of exposure is performed correctly, and this step is also easy if the photographer will remember a few simple rules. A short explanation of "why" should make the rules of "how" very much simpler.

The Range of Color Film

The range through which a black and white film will handle objects of varying brightnesses is about 1 to 130. But the range through which color processes will handle *colors* of varying brightnesses is 1 to 4! Quite a difference, that. Let us take as an example of a color process—Kodachrome. Kodachrome is made up essentially of three emulsions, each one contributing one primary color, the three together forming an image in full color. Since these emulsions are black and white, it is logical to assume that each one has about the same range to black and white objects as regular monochromatic film has. But since the exposure must be correct for each layer, while the light diminishes by $\frac{1}{3}$ in its passage through each coating, it is obvious that a slight error in exposure will be multiplied by 3 in its passage through each emulsion. This error therefore in-

Using the Meter for Color

creases with each succeeding layer, so that for the bottom coating it is 3 x 3 x 3 or 27 times as great as the error would be on a black and white film. This limits, in turn, the effective exposure range to about 1 : 4, as already mentioned.

It is obvious that the greatest care in exposure must be taken for the colored objects in the scene. For if the colors are correctly exposed, the much greater range of the film to black and white objects will take care of them automatically. One could compare this to a chain, the black and white objects being the strongest link and the colored ones the weakest. Therefore, for best results, the exposure of color film should be computed on the basis of the weakest member of the chain—the light reflected from those objects having color. *Black and white are not considered colors!*

Using the Meter

Since the exposure for color film must be quite exact, the most accurate method of using the meter is indicated—the brightness range method. Close-up readings are taken of the brightest and darkest colors in the scene and the normal arrow set halfway between these light values on the exposure guide dial. Remember, disregard all black and white objects!

With a Junior or Ciné meter, the two readings of the brightest and darkest colors should be taken, the two values *averaged* and that average value used in setting the meter. For example, the brightest color might have a value of 16, and the darkest, 10. The meter should be set at 13—the averaged value.

In taking the *close-up* reading, the meter should be held about the same distance away as the object's smallest dimension. To avoid casting a shadow of the meter onto the object, it may be necessary to hold the instrument at an angle to the direction from which the light is coming. With reasonable care, readings can be taken of objects as small as 2 or 3 inches across.

Sometimes it will be either necessary or desirable to take *substituted* readings. Instead of measuring the actual object, one similar to it can be substituted. The back of the photographer's hand makes a good substitute for the subject's face. A nearby grass plot, tree, or rock can be substituted for similar objects in the distance. Merely remember that in taking

25. Pictures like this are excellent subjects for color photographs, but correct exposure is essential for good results. The range of Kodachrome can be considered to be 1 to 4. This range is represented on the meter by the "A" and "C" positions.

these substituted readings, the objects should be lighted the same as the ones for which they were substituted.

This simple method of using the meter by taking close-up readings of the brightest and darkest colors will almost always yield a well exposed transparency of good color. But the exposure can be handled with even more control if the photographer wishes. He can expose particularly for a dark color, a medium color or a bright one. This control can be achieved through the use of the indications of the range of color film found on Weston Universal instruments (Models 715 & 650).

Indications of the Film Range

These two indications are the "A" and "C" positions. Color film has a range to color of 1 to 4, and the distance between these two positions is just 1 to 4. Therefore they become the limits of the color film range. These are most helpful to the serious photographer.

Out-of-doors, where the photographer cannot control his lighting, very seldom, if ever, will the scene color range be as short as the film color range. It follows that very seldom will he be able to expose correctly for everything in the scene. By the use of the "A" and "C" positions he can expose for the particular part of the scene in which he is interested.

The upper limit of the scene range is the brightest color (or highest light values as shown by the meter), and the upper limit of the film range is represented by the "C" position on

39

the exposure guide dial. The lower limit of the scene range is the darkest color (the lowest light value shown by the meter), and the lower limit of film range is shown by the "A" position.

It becomes apparent that if the principal part of the scene is in the darker parts, the exposure should be adjusted accordingly. This can be done by setting the "A" position opposite the reading of darkest color in the scene in which the photographer is interested. By so doing, he matches the lower limit of the scene. The dark colors will be correctly exposed and all others up to the limit of the film range.

Or he can expose for the bright colors by setting the "C" position opposite the brightest color reading in which he is interested—matching the upper limits. The third alternative is to balance the normal arrow by setting it halfway between the darkest and brightest colors and in doing this expose for the middle colors.

Use of "C" Position

It has been found that the most pleasing transparency will result from exposure for the brightest colors. If the meter user finds that the scene range is beyond the film range, he will obtain the best rendition of the scene by matching the upper limits—the "C" position opposite the brightest color. He can easily ascertain if the scene is beyond the film limits by balancing the normal arrow halfway between the darkest and brightest colors. If the two scene readings extend outside the "A" and "C" positions, the scene range exceeds the film range.

Of course, it would be a mistake to expose for the bright colors if the dark ones were of more interest; but usually the bright colors are the principal ones.

As in black and white photography, the photographer always tries to keep modelling in his highlights, even at the risk of losing the shadow detail, because he knows that the human eye is always attracted to the highlight of a picture first. If the highlight is correctly exposed, the transparency will be pleasing even if the shadows are underexposed. Of course, it would be very desirable to have both highlights and shadow correctly exposed, but this is not always possible.

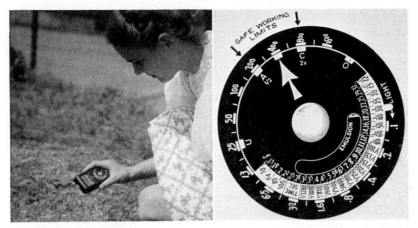

26, 27. (Left) Close-up readings of the various colors in the scene should be made. The meter should be held close enough to the object so that only it and nothing else is measured. (Right) In color photography, disregard all black and white objects, and use the brightness range method, considering only the colored objects.

When the principal subject is a human being, the flesh tones *must* be correctly, or at least pleasingly, rendered. We are so familiar with the color of human skin that we immediately detect a false flesh tone. At the expense of sacrificing other objects in the scene, the flesh colors should be exposed correctly.

When a scene is correctly lighted for a color photograph in which the subject is a human being, usually (in fact, almost always) the brightest color will be the highlight on the face. Best face tones will result in exposure for this brightest color by setting the "C" position opposite the sunlighted face reading.

If it is not possible to take a face reading or where it is not desirable, such as in a candid shot, the back of the photographer's sunlighted hand could be substituted. Here, then, is an excellent short-cut for color portraiture out-of-doors—merely take a meter reading from the back of your sunlighted hand, and most pleasing color rendition of the subject's skin tones will result by setting the "C" position opposite the hand light value.

Color Control Through Exposure

Some control over the color of a transparency can be effected through exposure. The more exposure given to a color, the lighter it will appear in the resulting transparency. Conversely, the less exposure, the darker the color. This is true because the lighter or darker negatives become darker or lighter color positives when reversed in the developing process. The use of varying exposures to vary colors is really only satisfactory when the scene to be photographed is made up of but one color, and perhaps a black or white object. For all the colors in the transparency would change together, and the only result would be an under- or over-exposure.

But with one color, particularly blue, some very convenient tricks can be played with its color shade. Visualize a scene of a brilliant white statue with a blue sky as a background. Here there is but one color, blue. The lightest shade of blue that could be achieved would be by means of the maximum correct exposure—the "C" block positioned so that it would be opposite the sky light value. The darkest shade of blue would result from a minimum correct exposure by setting the "A" position opposite the sky light value. Other shades of blue could be obtained by using any block between the "A" and "C" positions in setting the light value. The nearer the block used is to the "C" position, the lighter the color. The white statue, being white, is disregarded in computing the exposure.

Often, a dark blue sky as a background for a white object will be found very dramatic and a transparency made in this fashion will quickly attract attention where one with a normal blue sky is passed over. Most interesting applications of this exposure control can be made of snow-laden trees and cloudless skies. Incidentally, this is also a method of accentuating clouds where the transparency has as its subject only the cloud formations.

Color by Artificial Light

The exposure meter is handled for color by artificial light exactly the same as for sunlight. The same close-up readings and the same general suggestions apply for the setting of the dial. As in outdoor photography, the most pleasing color rendition of the scene will result by matching the "C" position to the brightest color.

Color film particularly matched to artificial illumination is available and this special material *must* be used. For movie makers and those with 35mm cameras, the film is intended for use with new photoflood lamps, while cut film users will find it necessary to use 3200°K lamps. The use of the wrong type of light will lead to unsatisfactory and off-color transparencies even though the exposure is perfect. It is said that rules are meant for artists to break—here is one the photographer must not break if he would have good color photographs.

As mentioned earlier, the range of color film is 1 to 4 as represented by the "A" and "C" positions on the exposure guide dial. Color photography by artificial light can be most satisfactory since the photographer can actually fit his scene to the film range through his lighting technique. The first step in making a color photograph by artificial light is to light the scene evenly with whatever type of lighting is indicated for the film in use— new photofloods for miniature and ciné cameras and 3200°K for cut film. The brightest color should then be measured and the "C" position set opposite the light value shown. Then measure the darkest color. If its light value falls on or within the "A" position, go ahead and take the picture. If the darkest color light value falls below the "A" position, additional light should be directed on it. When the scene range matches the film range, all colors will be satisfactorily rendered.

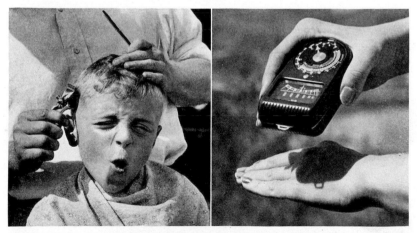

28, 29. (Left) A scene ideally suited to the use of the "C" position. A close-up reading is made of the sunlighted part of the boy's head, and the "C" position set to that value. (Right) In substituting the hand for a person's face, do not cast a shadow of the meter onto the hand. Here the girl is measuring the shadow, and the reading will not give the true value.

Color Temperature

For example, the picture under consideration might be a portrait. The steps to be followed would be:

1. Light the face as evenly as possible.
2. Measure the face highlight and set the "C" position opposite its light value.
3. Measure the darkest color (probably the hair).
4. Illuminate the darkest color so that its light value falls on or within the "A" position.

It would be noticed that the exposure is determined by the "C" position and brightest color, while the reproduction of the darker colors is controlled by their light value positions on the dial with respect to the "A" position.

Color Temperature

There are probably more sins in color photography committed in ignorance of the significance of color temperature than there are grains of silver in a photo-mural. What is color temperature? Imagine a block of iron, in the middle of a light-proof furnace. This piece of iron is being heated until it glows. When it reaches a temperature of 2000° in the Kelvin* scale, it emits light of a certain color quality. Any other light that has this same composition or color quality is said to have a color *temperature* of 2000°K. If the iron is heated to 3400°K. the composition of the emitted light will change and be much whiter. Any light whose composition (or *color*) matches that of the piece of metal heated to 3400°K. is said to have a color temperature of 3400°K. Incidentally that is the color temperature of a new photoflood lamp and the temperature for which 35mm Type A color film is balanced.

The higher the color temperature, the bluer the light, and the lower the temperature, the redder the light. Color film must be designed to operate for a definite light color composition. If the photographer wants satisfactory transparencies he must use the same light as that for which the film is balanced. With daylight film, he will use *sunlight;* with Type A material, *new* photofloods and with sheet-film, Type B—3200°K. lamps.

---

* The Kelvin scale is a measure of temperature just as is the Centigrade or Fahrenheit scale. A temperature of 2000° C. = 2273° K. Any temperature in degrees C. may be changed to degrees K. by adding 273° (approximately).

30, 31. (Left) Where there is but one color in the scene, all other objects being black or white as in this illustration, the normal arrow should be set to the light value of that color. (Right) If the principal object is white and stands out against the sky, the sky color can be varied by varying the exposure.

Why the insistence on *new* photofloods? Because as a photoflood is burned, the color of the light becomes more red—in other words, the color temperature drops. The two-hour lamps are good for color for the first 45 minutes of burning time, and the ten-hour bulbs are satisfactory for about 4 hours of burning time. After that they should be discarded or used only for black and white.

Out-of-doors in the daytime all light usually comes from the sun. Yet there is continual variation in color quality (temperature) of sunlight. Some place between the sun and the earth, the light has its color changed. On a bright day, when the sky is clear, the sunlight is perfect for color photographs. And proper exposure will result in pictures with excellent color rendition. But on a day where the sky is overcast, the light falling on the ground will be blue and hence the photograph will be too blue in spite of theoretically correct exposure.

The light in the shadow portions of the scene comes from the sky and, naturally, color pictures made with this shadow light will be blue—its color temperature is too high for the film. On the other hand, the light late in the afternoon or early in the morning will be too red for satisfactory color work—too low

45

a color temperature. That is why transparencies exposed late in the afternoon are always too yellowish red, and why people's faces look too red. In the photographic dark room, where the only light is red, all objects in the room are red because that is the color of the light falling on them. Remember that color film is balanced or adjusted for sunlight during the hours of 9 A. M. to 4 P. M. (approximately). Also remember that;

1. Gray days mean blue transparencies (color temperature too high).
2. Shadows mean blue transparencies (again, color temperature too high). Keep subjects in open sunlight.
3. Sunrises and sunsets are all right to take pictures of, but not *with*. They mean yellowish-red transparencies (color temperature too low).

Expose color film correctly to the correct light and avoid disappointments. Save the film when conditions are not right.

Color Reflections

Sometimes everything—exposure, light, and film—is right but still the color picture is unsatisfactory. This may be due to the fact that colored surfaces reflect light the same color as themselves. For example, the light reflected onto another surface by an orange background would be orange; a red surface would reflect red light; a blue one, blue, and so forth.

To avoid color reflections, be certain that the object being photographed is not too near colored surfaces or that these colored surfaces are not brilliantly lighted. For it is only logical that if no light falls on a surface, it can reflect none, colored or white.

Filters for Color Photography

It is obvious that the customary color filters used for black and white will not be satisfactory for color photography. A K-2 filter would make the color picture yellow because the filter removed all the blue from the light. A red one would make the picture red, and so forth for any filter used in black and white. But there are filters which are quite useful in color photography.

First, the haze filter. This filter is merely a means of correcting for excessive blue and ultraviolet in the light falling on the scene. It should be used on hazy days, for distant scenes or when in high altitudes. The haze filter requires no increase in exposure, hence the exposure meter is used in the regular manner recommended for color.

There is available a filter which enables the photographer to use Type A Kodachrome (balanced for tungsten) in daylight. This filter requires a change in exposure which is nicely taken care of by a change in the Weston emulsion rating. Type A Kodachrome, when used in daylight with a filter, should be exposed at Weston 8 instead of 12.

Pola-screens are, in effect, filters. They can be used in color work for darkening a blue sky without affecting the other scene colors. They require an increase in exposure, and being, in effect, neutral density filters, as contrasted to color correction filters, they can be compensated for by placing the filter, rotated as desired, in front of the cell of the meter and the reading taken through them. The meter is, of course, then used in the regular recommended manner. If the filter is too small to fully cover the cell, then the alternative is to mark the barrel of the Pola-screen with a series of marks, and by experiment find the correct filter factor. The emulsion speed of the film should be divided by the resultant factor and the number used in setting the emulsion speed on the exposure guide dial. (See page 65 on color filters.)

32. Bright clear days are best for color photographs of people. Have them look downward so the sun won't bother their eyes.

Errors in Color Exposure

Among the instruments available to insure accurate color renditions is a Color Temperature Meter. This instrument will tell the careful operator the color temperature of the light falling on the subject. If the temperature is other than that for which the film is balanced, compensation can be made by using a series of *color compensating* filters. These can be had for various color temperatures. But since they all act in the same manner as a haze filter (the haze filter is also color compensating) no change in exposure is necessary from that indicated by the meter.

Equipment Errors

Occasionally, the user of a meter will find that his transparencies are consistently over- or under-exposed. He will then recognize that the errors in his equipment are such as to show up in incorrect exposure. Shutters do not always (very seldom, as a matter of fact) actually operate at the marked speeds; lenses lose a certain amount of light in its transmission through the many pieces of glass in an optic so that the f-stop is not always actually as marked. Usually these and other errors cancel each other, but occasionally they will add in such a manner as to cause over- or under-exposure.

To compensate for these errors most conveniently, the photographer can change the rating of the film in accordance with the presented evidence. For example, the correct rating is 8 Weston. If the transparencies are consistently overexposed, the rating should be raised to 10 or 12 Weston. On the other hand, if under-exposure is constantly in evidence, the rating should be dropped to 6 or 4.

When starting color photography, it would be a good idea to take out an "insurance policy" by exposing a roll of film to various objects at film ratings ranging from 4 to 12. Then, upon inspection, the correct rating for the equipment could be arrived at.

Summary

1. Take close-up readings of the darkest and brightest *colors* in the scene.
2. Use the "A" and "C" position to expose for the objects of most interest.

3. Use only the light for which the film is balanced. Avoid placing the principal subjects in shadow; avoid gray days, and pictures early or late in the day (except *of* sunrises or sunsets).
4. Calibrate your equipment thru a changed film rating. This is usually not necessary, but better take out that insurance policy!

Exposure Experiments

1. Choose any scene, use the camera position method and expose a frame of Kodachrome accordingly.
2. Repeat using the darkest and brightest color method. Note the better reproduction obtained.
3. Choose a moderately long range scene and make three exposures as follows:
   a. "A" position set opposite darkest color light value.
   b. "C" position set opposite brightest color light value.
   c. Normal arrow balanced between the two.
   Note that the most pleasing picture results through the use of the "C" position.
4. Examine Kodachromes made on gray days and the parts of Kodachromes representing the shaded portions of the scenes. Note the blueness.
5. Make a color portrait late in the afternoon—see the Indian face!
6. Calibrate your camera by making exposures of a color chart as follows:
   a. Paste pieces of colored paper on a stiff cardboard.
   b. Set the chart in open sunlight.
   c. Take close-up readings of the various colors, then set the normal arrow midway between the darkest and brightest colors.
   d. Make six exposures at speeds of 4, 5, 6, 8, 10, 12.
   e. After processing, choose the exposure showing the best reproduction of the chart, and associate it with the speed at which it was exposed. All Kodachromes made with the camera used for the tests should then be exposed at this speed.

33. Portraits of people are usually more effective when the head and shoulders and sometimes part of the body fill the picture area. Otto F. Hess made this shot with the model four feet in front of a light background . . . one 500-watt spot directed from the right rear, one 500-watt No. 519 Britelite from the left front, and a No. 2 diffused photoflood almost in front of the camera. 1/5 second, f/16, Super Panchro Press film.

50

Portraiture

PRACTICALLY every amateur photographer has tried his hand at portraiture, and if he hasn't, he will shortly. The word "portraiture" can cover a multitude of sins. Even a snapshot of the wife, young lady-friend or brother can be classified as a portrait.

As in every other field of photography, the most important step in making a portrait is exposure, and as in these other fields, it must be correct. The surest way of obtaining correct exposure is by using the exposure meter and the brightness range method.

Remember, two close-up readings are taken, one of the brightest object and one of the darkest. Then the exposure is balanced halfway between by setting the normal arrow midway between the two readings. In the case of the Junior and Ciné meters, the two readings are averaged and the averaged value used to set the instrument.

Since, in portraiture, the photographer is usually primarily interested in the person being pictured, the background should be disregarded and the two readings taken from the subject. Usually the brightest object will be the highlight on the face, and the darkest object the hair. This is not an absolute rule. A sunlighted white shirt would be brighter than the face and a dark suit might be darker than the hair. But whatever the two extremes might be, the best exposure will be one centered midway between.

A few hints concerning outdoor portraiture might be wise. Let us list a few do's and don'ts.

1. Keep the lighting of the face soft and even. Frequently

a shaded face will result in a more pleasing portrait than one twisted and grimacing because of glaring sunlight.

2. Avoid distracting backgrounds, and don't insult the subject by allowing trees and telephone poles to grow out of his head.

3. Make the image of the subject quite large. When the photographer makes a portrait he wants to show a person, not a small dot on a landscape.

4. Try a few effects with sunlight. The "sun over your shoulder" is a good idea when you don't have a meter. Try backlighting a face—you can even put a halo around that favorite person of yours if you wish to obtain a dramatic effect.

5. Remember always that you are trying to picture an individual, hence avoid backgrounds and surroundings that might detract from the principal subject.

34. There are times when the background contributes to the atmosphere of the picture. The outdoor country atmosphere would be destroyed if the background were eliminated in this shot by Barbara Morgan.

35, 36. (Left) The subject will be most relaxed and normal if she is in the shade. The meter is used in the regular manner. (Right) Shading the eyes with a hat is an excellent way to avoid that "snapshot squint." Exposure for a portrait like this must be exact.

> 6. First, last and always—expose correctly by taking two readings from the darkest and brightest parts of the subject and centering the exposure halfway between.

For portraiture by artificial light, whether it be the formal type of the professional or the informal "snapshots at night" kind—the same exposure meter technique should be used as for outdoor work. Disregard the background, take two readings and center the exposure midway between.

Lighting Contrast

The professional is not the only one interested in making formal portraits; amateurs have also done a lot of work in this field. Perhaps the most difficult thing about formal portraiture for the amateur to master is the lighting of the face. It *is* difficult to judge lighting contrast without a lot of experience. But the exposure meter is, after all, a light meter and it can be used as a very convenient method of measuring light contrast. Naturally, a little experimentation will be necessary before the amateur can use his meter to the best advantage as a lighting guide.

53

37, 38. (Right) A gray day is easy on the subject. Waiting for the sun to go behind a cloud is a good substitute. Here, a few minutes wait for a cloud avoided eyestrain in the subject. (Left) The ratio of the light value of the shadow side of the face to the bright side is the contrast number. Duplication of lighting effects is easy if records are kept.

In making a formal portrait, the first thing to do is to light the face with a flood light. Usually this light (called the *source* light) will illuminate the face quite flatly or evenly. Hence, one side of the face will receive as much illumination as the other. Sometimes the photographer will want one side of the face brighter than the other. He will then use another light to illuminate only that side. By moving the light closer, or by utilizing a stronger one and directing it so that its illumination will fall on the desired part, the face will no longer be evenly illuminated. The ratio of the light reflected from one side to the other can be called the "lighting contrast." It is this that is so difficult to judge.

Instead of judging, a close-up reading should be taken from the brighter side, and one from the darker. By dividing the value obtained from the bright side by the one shown for the dark one, a numerical figure representing the lighting contrast can be obtained. For example, one side might yield a light value of 100 and the other, 25. The lighting contrast number would then be 4 (100 divided by 25). All other things being equal, the same result will always be arrived at in the future if the lighting contrast is adjusted to 4.

A different result would be arrived at if the contrast were 2, 3, 5 or 10. Any of these can be duplicated thru the use of a meter. A good idea for one just starting formal portraiture would be to take a series of pictures, varying the lighting and measuring it with the meter. If the shadow side always had a light value of 25, a lighting contrast of 2 would be obtained if the highlight side were 50 $\left(\frac{50}{25} = 2\right)$; a contrast of 3 if the highlight were 75; a contrast of 10 if the highlight were 250 and so forth.

After developing the negatives all for the same length of time, prints can be made and a whole series of effects will be shown. Any of these can be duplicated any time in the future by adjusting the lighting, measuring it with the meter and hence obtaining the same contrast number.

Usually the professional photographer will adjust his lighting contrast to 4. That is, the bright side of the face will be 4 times brighter than the dark side. He often will also add a back-light to put a bit of sparkle and luster in the subject's hair.

Many other variations of lighting can be used if desired; the suggested method is naturally only one general means. The exposure in any case is always based on the darkest and brightest parts of the subject.

High and Low Key Portraits

The usual portrait has a full scale of tones from black to white. A high key study is one in which most of the predominating tones are in the light gray or white end of the scale; a low key picture shows most of the tones in the dark gray or black end of the tone scale.

High and low key portraits are the result of lighting of the original subject and the printing of the negative. They have nothing to do with exposure; hence, the usual method recommended for portraiture should be used for these special effects.

Usually, the background is disregarded both in lighting and exposure in favor of the subject. Sometimes, however, it may be

Background Exposure

desirable to know beforehand what the tone of the background will be before the exposure is actually made. The Universal exposure meter can be used for this also.

Background Tone

On the exposure guide dial of the meter will be found two positions, the "U" and "O." The fundamental purpose of these two positions will be explained later on. For our purpose, they will aid the indication of the background tone.

After the exposure meter is set in accordance with the two close-up readings from the subject, a quick reading can be taken of the background. If the light value of the background falls on or near the "U" position, the background will be black in the final print. If the light value falls on or near the "O" position, the background will be white. And between these two positions will be various shades of gray.

After lighting and measuring the exposure, then the background can be taken care of. By illuminating the background with separate lights, any tone can be attained. Meter readings will show how the various background light values will result in different tones, and the nearer the value is to the "U" position, the darker it is, and the nearer to the "O" position, the lighter.

Summary

1. For portraiture, informal or formal, indoors or out, the exposure meter should be used by taking readings of the darkest and brightest parts of the subject and centering the exposure halfway between.
2. The meter can be used to measure light contrast and by means of a "contrast number" effects can be duplicated.
3. While the background is usually disregarded, its tone can be controlled by using the meter.

Exposure Experiments

1. Make a series of four portraits such that the lighting contrast numbers on the face are 1, 2, 4, and 8.
2. Develop all for the same time and print on the same grade of paper. Note the differences among them. File for future reference.

Motion Picture Photography

THE many millions of persons in this country who use personal motion picture cameras have found that they can make or break their movies by the exposure settings they use. Many of them have taken their cue from the professional cinematographers and added an exposure meter to their equipment.

Before considering exposure, let us examine a ciné camera. It has a series of f/ stops marked on its lens and a shutter which admits the light to the film. A control of quantity and a control of duration, the same as a still camera! As a matter of fact, the only difference between a still and ciné camera is that the still camera takes but one picture while the ciné one makes a number each second. The controls of exposure being the same in each case, the use of the exposure meter is identical for ciné photography as for still.

Special Ciné Exposure Meters

The shutter speed of the usual motion picture camera is usually limited to one at 16 frames per second. Frames per second, of course, refers to the number of pictures exposed each second. Some cameras have a variable number of frames per second feature, but the normal number is usually 16. Since there is not the choice of a number of f-stop—shutter speed combinations, it is possible to simplify the exposure meter when it is to be used solely for ciné photography. The Model 720 Master Ciné meter is an example.

Here the exposure guide dial can be preset to the film rating, the number of frames per second at which the camera is operating, and the camera class, or type. Then the meter is practically direct reading, for opposite the light reading value on the exposure guide dial will be found the correct f-stop. The type of camera is determined by the speed of the shutter at 16 frames per second. A Type A camera is one having a speed of 1/25 to 1/35 of a second, while a Type B machine has a speed of 1/40 to 1/50 of a second.

The Ciné meter should be used exactly as a Universal type of instrument. For general use, the meter should be aimed at the middle of the scene, aimed halfway between the horizon line and your feet. Then merely read off the correct f-stop. The brightness range method can be used by taking a close-up reading of the darkest and brightest objects in the scene. After averaging the two readings, the correct f-stop will be found opposite the averaged value. For color, the two reading method must be used, but the two objects measured would of course be the darkest and brightest colors.

Universal Exposure Meters

Since the ciné camera is the same as a still one, the universal exposure meter is used in exactly the same manner for movies as for stills. But instead of having a series of f-stop—shutter speed combinations, there is only one combination that is correct. The first step is to find out the speed at which your camera operates at 16 frames per second. For example, it may be 1/30 of a second. After setting the exposure guide dial, the correct f-stop would then be found opposite 1/30 of a second. If it were 1/40 or 1/50, then their corresponding f-stops would be used.

Other Frames per Second

Some ciné cameras are able to expose film at speeds other than 16 frames per second. These more complete instruments might be able to expose film at 8, 16, 24, 32, or 64 frames per second. The effect on the exposure is obvious. If a smaller number of pictures are exposed each second, each picture or frame would have a greater exposure. Conversely, if a greater number than 16 were exposed during the second interval, each frame would have correspondingly less exposure. With a ciné type of meter, the instrument is set according to the number of frames per second at which the camera is operating. But with the Universal meter, a different type of compensation is necessary.

39. As far as exposure is concerned, a movie camera is the same as a still one. The picture would be exposed the same in either case.

As was seen before, the effect of lowering the number of frames per second is to increase the exposure for each frame. If a camera has a shutter speed of 1/30 of a second at 16 frames per second, the speed would effectively be 1/15 of a second at 8 frames per second since the one second interval would be split up among 8 frames instead of 16—and each frame would be exposed twice as long. At 32 frames per second, the interval would be spread over twice as many frames, and naturally each frame would be exposed only one half as long. The shutter speed in the above example would therefore be 1/60 of a second.

59

Calculating True Shutter Speed

If the camera were operating at 8 frames per second, the f-stop opposite 1/15 of a second would be the correct one, and if operating at 32 frames, the f-stop opposite 1/60 of a second would be correct. These are, of course, correct only for the above example where the speed at 16 frames is 1/30.

A general rule expressed mathematically, which can be applied to all cameras, is as follows:

$$\frac{16}{\substack{\text{Frames per second} \\ \text{at which camera} \\ \text{is operating}}} \times \substack{\text{Shutter speed} \\ \text{at 16 frames}} = \substack{\text{TRUE SHUTTER} \\ \text{SPEED}}$$

For example, the camera may be operating at 32 frames per second, and the original speed at 16 frames may be 1/40 of a second—$\frac{16}{32} \times \frac{1}{40} = 1/80$. Listed below will be found a table for cameras having speeds of 1/30, 1/40, and 1/50 of a second.

No. Frames	1/30	1/40	1/50
8	1/15	1/20	1/25
16	1/30	1/40	1/50
24	1/45	1/60	1/75
32	1/60	1/80	1/100
48	1/90	1/120	1/150
64	1/120	1/160	1/200

If the meter does not show a speed exactly the same as the one at which the camera is actually operating, the nearest value should be used. For example, 1/45 can be considered to be 1/40 without noticeable or measurable error.

40. A cine meter guide dial can be preset to camera type, frames per second and film rating.

It will be noticed that the effective shutter speed can be varied by varying the number of frames per second. It may be necessary to make use of this where the illumination is insufficient to make an exposure at the normal speed of 16 frames. Then 8 or even 6 frames may be indicated. If the f-stop opposite the shutter speed is too large (numerically small) for your camera, try the equivalent speed at 8 frames per second— that is, of course, if your camera can operate at that number of frames. Perhaps the resulting slower speed will enable you to make the picture. If the f-stop indicated is still too large— *Don't Take The Picture!*

The exposure meter is just as useful to the cinematographer to tell him when a picture is not possible as it is to tell him the correct f-stop. If the meter says "no picture," don't waste the film. Sometimes the meter will indicate an f-stop smaller than that with which your camera is equipped. The solution here is to use a slower film, a color filter or both. Again—if it is not possible to set the camera to the f-stop indicated by the meter, forget the whole thing and save your film.

Cameras are equipped with variable number of frames per second fundamentally to adjust the speed of action on the screen. To slow up the action, 32, 48, or 64 frames per second should be used, while 8 or 6 frames should be used to speed up action. Sometimes these variable frame speeds can be used to make a picture possible when no other course is open. This change is not recommended if it is possible to avoid it.

Panning is one thing that a ciné camera can do that sometimes affects exposure which does not concern the still photographer. This is true when the photographer pans from a bright to dark part of the scene, or vice versa. A particularly good example of this is the shipboard pictures that every ciné fan makes as soon as he gets over his seasickness when on a cruise. Here the bright light intensity of the open deck requires an exposure materially different from that needed in the portions shaded by an upper deck.

It is obvious, therefore, that before the cinematographer pans, he should measure the exposure for all parts of the scene, and when the camera views a portion of the scene of changed light intensity, the exposure should be changed.

Ciné Meters for Still Cameras

Acceptance Angles

Some amateurs have felt that since the ciné camera views a smaller area than does the still camera, some restrictions should be put on the exposure meter. This is true up to a certain point. The meter should have a narrow viewing (or acceptance) angle, and the Weston Master meters are designed to have this small angle. But it is not necessary to have the angle agree exactly.

In general, the Ciné type meters have smaller acceptance angles than the regular Universal types have. The reason is that a smaller angle can be achieved because the ciné meter does not need the great sensitivity required for still photography, hence some sensitivity can be sacrificed to attain the smaller angle.

Above all, do not try to restrict the viewing angle of your meter with an outside extra mask or tube. This would change the calibration and make the instrument highly inaccurate.

Ciné Meters and the Still Camera

Those who take both ciné and still pictures should obtain a Universal instrument which can be used for both. But sometimes the man who uses only the ciné camera finds himself required to make a few snapshots. This might happen only twice a year, and he will not want to sacrifice the convenience of the special meter for these infrequent occasions. His ciné meter can be used to guide him in still photography as follows:

1. Set film rating and the guide dial to a Type B camera.
2. Decide on the shutter speed to be used. And set the meter to a number of frames per second as follows:

Shutter speed desired	No. Frames
1/25	8
1/50	16
1/100	32
1/150	48
1/200	64

3. The meter is then direct reading for the shutter speed selected. In other words, if the meter is set for 8 frames, the meter will indicate the f-stop at 1/25 of a second— at 16 frames, 1/50 and so forth.

41. A ciné meter can be used with a still camera for a scene of this kind. Set the meter for a "type B" camera and use the f-stop directly opposite 1/50 second.

The average still will probably be exposed at 1/50 of a second, hence the meter will indicate the f-stop needed by setting the dial to 16 frames—the one usually used.

Summary

1. Exposure meters are used in the same manner for ciné photography as for still, because still and ciné cameras are essentially the same from an exposure viewpoint.
2. The shutter speed of a ciné camera is dependent upon the inherent design of the camera and upon the number of frames per second at which it operates.
3. When panning, the exposure should be changed in accordance with changed light in various parts of the scene.
4. The acceptance angles of the meter and camera do not have to be exactly the same, but a small angle is a desirable meter characteristic.

63

42. The effectiveness of this picture was materially increased through the use of a K2 filter.

Color Filters

THE light which is most generally used to make pictures is made up of all the colors in the spectrum, the combination resulting in white. Various objects in the scene are colored by their absorption of part of this white light and reflection of the remainder. For example, a rose is red because it reflects red light and absorbs all others; the color of an object depends on what colors it absorbs. When the shutter of the camera clicks, the film is acted upon not by the original white light that fell on the scene, but the part that was reflected from the scene and this light is colored—green, blue, red, etc.

Regular black and white film is more sensitive to some colors than to others; hence for a given amount of reflected light one object may appear darker or lighter in the finished picture than it was to the eye, because of this varying sensitivity of the film. For the usual run of photographs where only a record of the scene is desired, this somewhat false monochromatic rendering of the scene is perfectly satisfactory. But sometimes the photographer may wish to control the relative gray tone values of the colors in the scene, and to do this he uses color filters.

The filter is usually a piece of colored glass or gelatine which is placed in front or back of the lens. It acts somewhat like a sieve, allowing some colors to pass through onto the film, and keeping back others. A color filter will always allow its own color to pass through in the greatest percentage and keep back its complementary. For example, a red filter will allow all red light from the scene to pass onto the film, but it will "strain" or filter out all green light. The result is that all red objects in the scene will appear lighter in the finished photograph than would ordinarily be the case, and all green objects, darker.

Exposure Compensation for Filters

Since some of the light from the scene is "strained" out before it reaches the film, the exposure must be greater than the exposure meter would indicate. The necessary increase varies with the color and shade of the filter and with each film emulsion. The number of times increase in exposure for each combination has been calculated by the film manufacturer and is called a *Filter Factor*.

The easiest method of compensation in exposure when a color filter is used is to divide the emulsion speed rating of the film in use by the filter factor. The resultant number is then used to set the exposure meter.

Some photographers have felt that by placing the filter over the cell of the exposure meter, the necessary increase in exposure would automatically be taken care of. The difficulty with this is that the factor of a given filter will vary with the film being used. For example, a K_2 yellow filter might have a factor of 2 with a panchromatic emulsion, and a factor of 4 with an orthochromatic one. The meter cannot tell what kind of film is being used, hence a great error might be introduced. Incidentally, without a filter, this difference in color sensitivity of film is taken care of by the film rating.

So, to take care of filter factors—divide the emulsion rating of the film in use by the filter factor. For example, the emulsion rating might be 24 and the filter factor, 2. Dividing 24 x 2, the result is 12. Hence, 12 is used to set the exposure guide dial.

Using Filters

A filter is most often used to accentuate clouds and darken skies in doing so. Usually a light or medium yellow filter is used to do this with filter factors ranging from 1.5 to 4.0 depending upon the shade of the color and the film being used. There are other uses, and for convenience we will list various filters and a few recommended uses. Wratten filters will be used as examples; similar colors in filters made by others can also be used.

Wratten	Color	Use
K_1	light yellow	For slight correction by subduing some blue in the scene. To accentuate clouds and bring out texture in snow scenes.

43. Clouds can be accentuated and a landscape with very little subject matter should be photographed through the use of suitable filters. Photo by Vachon from Farm Security Administration.

K_2	medium yellow	More correction by subduing considerably more blue than the K_1. Usually used when clouds are to be brought out sharply and still preserve naturalness. Excellent for snow scenes.
K_3	deep yellow	Still more correction. Blues will register even darker.
G	orange yellow	Excellent for distant scenes since the G filter has good haze-cutting qualities. This filter is also useful in eliminating yellow stains from old prints when copying.
X_1	light green	In daylight, it allows the film to respond to color similarly to the human eye. Its use will have a good effect on the shadow detail of

67

		greens. Can be substituted for a K_2 filter and its effect on the sky is practically the same
X_2	medium green	Used with Type C pan in tungsten light to make the film respond to color as the human eye does. Not recommended for other purposes.
F	cherry red	For infra-red work and to eliminate all blue light reaching the film. The use of the F filter will result in black skies. Very effective for some subjects, particularly white ones. A so-called contrast filter.
A	medium red	Can be used in place of the F filter and for direct color separations. Passes only red light.
B	green	Direct color separation—passes only green light.
C_5	dark blue	Direct color separation—passes only blue light.

Only the most useful filters have been listed; there are hundreds of shades and colors for every specialized purpose. But all are used in exactly the same manner as far as the exposure meter is concerned. Divide the film speed rating by the filter factor.

For Special Effects

Sunset photographs are very effective. Usually they are composed of some attractive object silhouetted against a clouded sky. A K_2, G or F filter should be used and the exposure based only upon the light coming from the sky. The meter should be pointed directly at the setting sun and at the zenith. The normal arrow should then be set halfway between. With the Junior or Ciné meters, the two values should be averaged and the average figure used to set the meter. This, of course, applies to sunrises as well as sunsets—or any other time when the sky is to be featured and a silhouette made.

If the figures in the foreground or the landscape are such that it is desirable to have detail in them, the proper filter should be used, the sky disregarded, and the exposure based upon the figures or landscape in the regular manner.

When the filter is to be used merely to correct the monochromatic rendering of the scene, the meter is used in the regular fashion and correction is made on the emulsion rating for the filter factor. This also applies to direct color work, but in this case the recommendations found in the chapter on color should be followed.

Don't use a filter when it is unnecessary to do so. Just as many photographs fail because a filter is unnecessarily used as for want of one.

Exposure Experiments

1. Take four pictures of the same landscape using the following filters, compensating for filter factors: K_2, G, X and F.
2. Develop all four negatives for the same time. Print on the same grade of paper. Note the differences in reproduction of the various colors in the scene.

44, 45. (Left) Filters can be used to control tones. Here the blue flower of the thistle is rendered almost white through the use of a blue filter. (Right) Everyday subjects can be made interesting by deliberate under-exposure resulting in a silhouette like this.

46. Close-up readings should be made for beach scenes to avoid the influence of the specular reflection of the sand.

Specular vs. Diffuse Brightness

A FAMOUS philosopher once said, "If you would talk with me, define your terms." To avoid confusion, let us define the terms "Specular" and "Diffuse."

Some surfaces such as water, glass, polished metal, etc. reflect light in a definite direction which depends upon the direction of the source of the light, the angle of reflection being equal to the angle of incidence. This type of reflection is known as *specular*.

Other surfaces, crystalline in structure, such as chalk, magnesium oxide, etc. reflect light falling upon them by scattering it in all directions. This is known as *diffused* reflection.

Then there are still other surfaces, such as sand, snow, rough water, etc. which produce both specular and diffused reflection. That is, while the reflected light is more or less diffused, there are certain directions where the reflected light is greater than from others.

It follows that a surface which sparkles to the eye will be specular when the light is reflected directly into the eye and will be diffuse if viewed from an angle such that the surface does not appear to sparkle.

The exposure meter is calibrated to measure diffuse brightness, and seeing things much like the eye, will be affected by specular reflections. The meter will measure the bright sparkles and the resulting exposure will be correct for them. But the darker parts of the scene will be underexposed. Therefore, a surface which sparkles to the eye should not be metered from the same direction that the picture is to be made.

71

How Sand and Water Affect Exposure

Instead, the photographer should turn around and measure the surface in such a fashion that the sun is coming over his shoulder. With the light falling on the scene from behind the photographer, the surface will be changed to a diffuse one for which the meter is calibrated and correct exposure will be obtained.

Now let us consider a few types of scenes in which specular surfaces might be present:

Beach Scenes

Sand is a particularly good example of a semi-specular surface, for it is crystalline in structure and in common with most crystalline substances it reflects light as a mirror, or directionally. When the light is such that it is backlighting the scene, the photographer should turn around so that the scene measured by the meter will be flatly illuminated. If the beach as the photographer wishes to photograph it is already flatly illuminated, the sand will not, of course, act as a specular surface and he will not need to change his technique.

47. Here is a semi-specular surface, one which sparkles to the eye and to the camera. The camera position reading would be wrong here.

48. The combination of ice, water and backlighting made it necessary to use the brightness range method for this picture.

Snow Scenes

Snow acts in exactly the same manner as sand; that is, it acts as a semi-specular surface because snow flakes are crystals. Usually the most effective snow pictures are made when the scene is backlighted. That means there will be specular reflections present. Two ways of using the meter would present themselves:

1. A general camera position reading taken in the opposite direction from that in which the picture is to be made. The "C" position should be used because the scene would be a contrasty or long range one.
2. The brightness range method. A shadowed tree would probably be the darkest object and the sunlighted snow the brightest. When taking the snow reading, the sun should be over the photographer's shoulder.

Diffusely illuminated snow scenes would not have specular reflections, therefore no precautions need be taken.

Water and Over-water Scenes

Backlighted water is also specular in character, and the same recommendations are made for the photography of water as for sand and snow.

When the objects of interest are on the other side of, or on a river or lake, and the scene is backlighted, the brightness range

73

method employing substituted nearby objects should be used. If the scene is illuminated with flat light, a simple camera position reading will be satisfactory.

Rainy Weather Pictures

Wet pavements act as specular surfaces, but during the daytime when pavements are wet they are usually wet because it is raining, and then, of course, there isn't any sunlight to make them sparkle. But at night, street lights can cause specular reflections. The lack of general light makes the usual type of correction impossible. Two courses of action are open:

1. Measure the specular surfaces and use the normal arrow setting. This will correctly expose the bright sparkling portions of the scene and usually underexpose the shadows. The result will often be a rather striking effect.
2. Measure the bright surfaces and use the "O" position in setting the dial. To do this, merely set the "O" position opposite the light value obtained. If a Junior meter is being used, the setting should be made in the regular fashion and the selected shutter speed multiplied by eight.

Summary

1. Most surfaces of objects the photographer meets are diffuse in that the reflected light rays are scattered in all directions. The meter is calibrated for the resulting diffuse brightness.
2. Some, however, which sparkle to the eye, are specular. The meter readings of these surfaces should be taken with the light source back of the photographer's shoulder.
3. The specular materials most often met with are sand, snow, water, glass and unpainted metals.

Exposure Experiments

1. Make two pictures of a back lighted water, snow, or beach scene. Expose one in accordance with the meter used from the camera position, the other as recommended in this chapter.
2. Develop and print the two the same way. Note the underexposure in the first picture made.

Additional Applications

THE general methods of using an exposure meter described before are, of course, applicable to all fields and types of photography. But in some specialized fields, there are little tricks which will make correct exposure easier of attainment.

Copying

When making copies of other photographs or of screen cuts, the photographer must work carefully to be able to reproduce the tones of the original in the copy. This means correct exposure and correct development; also the correct film for the purpose.

The author has found that moderately slow films like Defender Fine Grain Panchromatic or Eastman Commercial Pan are ideal. With the pan film, filters can be used when necessary and the material will yield excellent reproduction of the original tone values. Never use a high speed film for copying. High speed is not necessary; hence it is more logical to choose the slower material with more desirable reproduction characteristics.

When copying line drawings, diagrams or printed matter, a process film is indicated. Regular process film will often have enough contrast to yield a black and white copy devoid of any middle tones. But for the utmost in contrast for either black on white, or white on black, Agfa Reprolith or Eastman Kodalith will be ideal. *Do not* use these films for continuous tone copies where half and middle tones are necessary.

Exposure in line work can easily be measured by substituting a piece of white paper for the material to be copied and

taking the meter reading close-up to the paper. Then the normal arrow should be used in setting the light value. In taking
the close-up reading be careful not to cast a shadow of the meter
on the paper

Incidentally, the smallest f-stop with which the diaphragm
is marked should be used, not so much to increase the actual
sharpness of the lens, but to compensate for any possible errors
in focusing. After exposure, the film should be processed in the
developer recommended by the film manufacturer for the length
of time and at the temperature indicated by him.

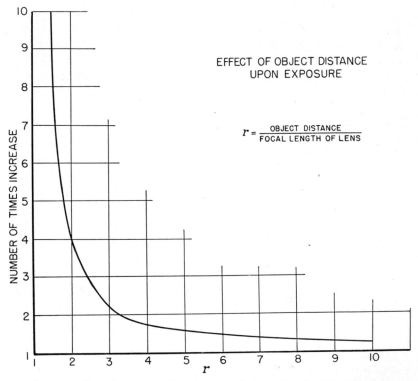

EFFECT OF OBJECT DISTANCE
UPON EXPOSURE

$$r = \frac{\text{OBJECT DISTANCE}}{\text{FOCAL LENGTH OF LENS}}$$

NUMBER OF TIMES INCREASE

r

49. Compensation of exposure for close-up photography. In general exposures
should be modified when subjects are closer than 8 times the focal length of the
lens employed.

Example: When an object is 10 inches from a 5 inch lens: $r = \frac{10}{5} = 2.$
Where the curve in the chart intersects the vertical line above "2"—
follow horizontal line to the left. It indicates "4": meaning 4 times
the normal exposure.

When making copies, the camera is usually quite close to the object, hence the lens does not operate at the f-stop marked on its barrel. The f-stop is a function of the diameter of the lens aperture and the distance of the lens from the film. When the lens-to-film distance is other than that for which the f-stop has been calculated (the focal length of the lens), the f-stop markings are no longer correct.

There are several ways of compensating for this error. One method is through the use of the accompanying curve. The distance from the camera to the object (called the object distance) is measured and the figure divided by the focal length of the lens to be used. The resultant number will be indicated by the letter R. Using the curve, the value for the exposure increase can be picked off the vertical axis. For example, as in the illustration, R was found to be 2. The figure 2 is found on the horizontal axis and by reading opposite the point where 2 occurs on the curve, a value of 4 is found. Hence the shutter speed indicated by the exposure meter should be multiplied by 4.

The Eastman Kodak Company publishes a small calculator dial for the same purpose. It is very convenient and easy to use and sells for ten cents. With this guide, the lens-to-the-film is measured (called the *image* distance) and this figure set opposite the value for the focal length of the lens in use. In a small window at the bottom of the dial, the exposure increase is shown. If the figure 2 appears, the time of exposure indicated by the meter should be multiplied by 2. Both systems work well; use either you choose.

With Junior and Ciné type exposure meters, the reading should be taken of the white paper as recommended for the Universal models and the meter set in the regular fashion.

Table-Tops

For this fascinating branch of photography, the brightness range method will be the best assurance of correct exposure. If the objects in the table-top setup are too small to measure, convenient larger objects can be temporarily substituted for them and the light reading taken from them. For example, when photographing a black cigarette case, a black plate holder could be substituted for the case in order to obtain the light reading for the black case.

Title Making

If the camera is close to the subject, as is usually the case for table-top studies, the same exposure compensation for additional extension must be made as in copying.

50, 51. (Left) Flower pictures are easy. Take a close-up reading of the flower and set the normal arrow at the light value. (Right) In action pictures take exposure reading before the event takes place by a general reading or by the substitution method where required, as in this photo.

Title Making

This is the movie-makers' equivalent of copying for the still photographer. A piece of white paper should be substituted for the copy material and the close-up reading taken of it. The normal arrow is used to set the exposure guide dial. This is for black and white movies. For Kodachrome titles, the reading should be made close-up to the original title material, and the normal arrow used in setting the dial. Caution again!—avoid the meter shadow!

Action Pictures

When making photographs of athletic events, or wherever the exposure must be made "on the fly," the general camera position reading should be taken before the anticipated action occurs. Then, when the picture presents itself, the photographer will be all set for it.

52. In title-making a piece of white paper is substituted for the copy material and a close-up reading taken.

When using color film, the brightness range method can be utilized by using substituted objects. For athletic events, the easiest way of using the meter for color is to take a reading from the back of your sunlighted hand, set the "C" position to the indicated value, adjust the camera and be ready to make the picture when the desired action occurs.

53. By taking a reading of the rock, and setting the "U" position to that light value, the minimum correct exposure will be secured.

79

54, 55. (Left) If all variables are not correctly correlated, the darkest object method may lead to underexposure and a bad picture. This picture was developed in a special fine grain developer with a resulting loss in film speed. (Right) The building in this picture was not accessible to the photographer for a close-up reading. Since the brightest object in the scene was a sunlighted rock, he found one close at hand, set the "O" position to the light value, and hence made use of the brightest object method.

Aerial Photography

Since photographs made of the earth from the air are almost always of flat scenes, there should be no difficulty in exposure. For, as you remember, there is great latitude in exposure to flat or short range scenes. The earth's surface from the air is photographically flat or short ranged because of the distance from it to the camera. A simple camera position reading from the plane and the use of the normal arrow is quite sufficient. If there is considerable atmospheric haze, there may be a tendency toward higher readings. Under these conditions, the "C" position could be used to set the calculator dial to advantage.

When taking the meter reading, take care not to include any of the airplane in which you are flying. Also, if an Aero filter is used, remember to compensate for it.

For photographs of cloud formations from the air, the meter should be aimed directly at them, but in a direction away from the sun. Again, the normal arrow setting will be satisfactory.

If the subject of the photograph from the air is another airplane, the meter reading could be obtained by aiming the meter at the wing of the plane in which you are flying. Or a meter reading could be taken of a plane when you were still on the ground if you knew that among your pictures was to be one of another airplane.

Underwater Photography

Light is just as variable underwater as overwater and on land. Usually when photographing underwater, the photographer is in some sort of diving bell, or its equivalent, such as a glass bottomed boat. The exposure meter should be pointed at the scene through the camera porthole or glass bottom, the normal arrow set to the light value, and the exposure adjusted accordingly.

Some underwater pictures must be made without the benefit of a diving bell or boat. Waterproof housings for the meter will take care of these circumstances—a glass in front so that the photographer can read the light value, and a glass in the rear so that the underwater light can reach the cell is all that is necessary.

Do not use the meter underwater *without* a suitable waterproof housing.

Latitude, Longitude and Altitude

Some photographers have asked if it were necessary to make compensation on the meter indications when the photographs were being made in the tropics or high in the mountains. This, of course, is entirely unnecessary, for the meter responds in the same way as the photographic film. If, in the tropics or on mountain tops, the light is very intense, the exposure must be shorter than usual. But the meter will indicate a higher light value than usual and the result will be the necessary shorter exposure. This applies irrespective of latitude, longitude and altitude.

81

56. The "U" position represents the darkest object correctly exposed, and the "O" the brightest. Between the "U" and "O" positions can be found all the densities which the negative is capable of producing. Photo by J. C. Allen and Son.

The U and O Positions

Wᴇ have discussed the use of the "A" and "C" positions and the normal arrow found on the exposure guide of the universal exposure meter. There are also two other positions on this dial, the "U" and "O."

To understand the use of these two positions, it will be necessary to understand the range of photographic film. As discussed before, correct exposure occurs when there is the right amount of light falling on the film in relation to the film's inherent sensitivity, so that the film can separate tone values. In other words, correct exposure occurs when the film yields two different densities for two objects of close, but different light intensities. When there is too little light to separate tones, all objects are recorded as clear film. When there is too much light, all objects are recorded in the maximum density of which the film and developer combination are capable. There is one point at which correct exposure starts, and another at which it stops. The former is represented by the letter "U" and the latter by the letter "O" on the exposure guide dial. The range between these two positions is the range of an average black and white film—1 to 128.

Of course, not all films have an actual range of 1 to 128, but in general that is a safe working figure. The value 1 to 128 means that if the darkest object in the scene has a given light intensity, the film will be able to expose correctly all other objects having light intensities up to and including those 128 times as brilliant.

The Darkest Object

Since there are indications of the film range on the exposure meter, they can be used to calculate correct exposure. One method of doing so makes use of the "U" position. It is perfectly logical to assume that the darkest object in the scene, being the last possible object in which separation is desired, can be correctly exposed for if the "U" position is set opposite its light value. By so doing, the photographer matches the lower light limit of the scene, the darkest object, with the lower limit of the film range, the "U" position. We will call this the darkest object method of using the Universal exposure meter.

As you will learn, the speed of film is affected by development technique, and since the darkest object method is working at the extreme limit of the film range, it would be wise to adjust speed ratings to your own processing conditions. Find, in the range of speeds for a given film, that rating which suits your developing technique. Not to do so may lead to unsatisfactory negatives resulting from the use of this method.

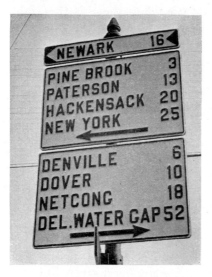

57. Claims of greatly increased film speed with special developers are true if short range scenes are chosen. This was exposed at 10X the true film speed, but who wants to make pictures of signs?

58. Film density strip—illustrative of the range of film.

59. Flat scenes will also be correctly exposed at higher than rated film speeds.

The advantages of the darkest object method are many, among them being:

1. The minimum correct exposure will result.
2. The minimum exposure will allow the maximum shutter speed to stop all motion.
3. A minimum f/ stop (the smallest possible under the lighting circumstances) for the greatest possible depth of field.
4. Accuracy of exposure where the brightness range method cannot be utilized because of the inaccessability of the brightest object.

To reiterate, the darkest object method will be satisfactory only if the emulsion rating of the film in use has been adjusted to your own developing technique.

The Brightest Object

Just as the "U" position can be matched to the darkest object light value, so can the "O" position be set opposite the

Brightness Range Limitations

brightest object light value. When this is done, the upper limit of the scene range is matched to the upper limit of the film range. Using the "U" position, the lower limits were matched, and just as logically, using the "O" position, the upper limits can be matched.

When these upper limits are matched, the maximum correct exposure results. Using the brightest object method, the photographer takes a close-up reading of the brightest object in the scene and then sets the "O" position opposite the brightest object light value.

This method should be used only when the scene is extremely dimly lighted. Under these circumstances, the brightness range method cannot be used because the darkest object is too dark for the meter to measure, and an over-all camera position reading might also be impossible because of the lack of illumination.

60, 61. (Two shots) For normal and long range scenes, increased speeds cannot be used regardless of the kind of developer. The picture on the left was exposed at the recommended speed and developed in accordance with recommended practice. The one on the right was exposed at an increased speed and developed in a solution supposedly intended for such underexposure.

86

62. Where the subject is apt to be restless, the minimum exposure obtained by the darkest object method will be found helpful.

Sometimes even the brightest object in the scene will be too dark to measure. Then a piece of white paper or a white handkerchief can be inserted into the scene and the close-up reading taken of that. If there is still too little illumination artificial light should be resorted to.

Controlling Negative Density

Since the use of the "U" position set opposite the darkest object light value will yield the minimum correct exposure, and the "O" position set opposite the brightest object light value the maximum correct exposure, it would follow that the thinnest negative correctly exposed would result from the use of the darkest object method, and the densest negative correctly exposed from the use of the brightest object method. This fact can be used effectively to control negative density.

63. Any picture will be improved by controlled development. Textures and detail are apparent in all parts of this scene because the negative density range matched the paper range.

87

Various Correct Exposures

64. Although this may be an interesting picture, it is technically poor. The negative was correctly exposed but overdeveloped, hence there was no paper available to match its great range. The result is black shadows.

Consider the illustration, page 84, fig. 58. It shows every photograph that has ever been made and every one possible for the future. It is a gray scale, illustrating the range, and hence all densities possible, from the darkest to the brightest object that can be handled by the film emulsion. If this range of the scene just meets the range of the film, only one exposure is possible, and that is the one shown on the exposure guide dial when the "U" position is opposite the darkest object light value, and the "O" position opposite the brightest light value.

But where the scene has a shorter range than the film, several exposures, all correct, can be used. If a dense negative is desired, the "O" position can be set opposite the brightest light value. If a thin negative is wanted, the "U" position should be set opposite the darkest light value. And if an average negative is wanted, balance the normal arrow midway between the two extremes.

Why Control Negative Density?

65. Controlled Development should be given to Correctly Exposed negatives. The PHOTO-LAB-INDEX by Henry M. Lester offers such Time-Gamma-Temperature Development Charts for some 250 Film-Developer Combinations. (See page 100).

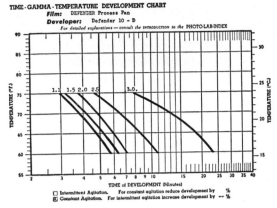

TIME - GAMMA - TEMPERATURE DEVELOPMENT CHART
Film: DEFENDER Process Pan
Developer: Defender 10 - D
For detailed explanations — consult the INTRODUCTION *to the* PHOTO-LAB-INDEX

☐ Intermittent Agitation. For constant agitation reduce development by %
☒ Constant Agitation. For intermittent agitation increase development by -- %

Why bother with this? Why control negative density? Frankly, there is no necessity for doing so. But if the photographer intends to enlarge his negatives, it will be convenient and helpful to have correctly exposed, thin negatives to work with. If the print is to be made by contact printing, a denser negative will be preferred. There is no real necessity for negative overall density control, but it does makes the printing of the negative more convenient.

66, 67, 68. Two negatives were used to make these three prints. One was correctly exposed and overdeveloped. In picture at left, the print was exposed for shadow detail; the next for highlight detail. The range of the negative made it impossible to get both. The picture at the right was printed from a negative correctly exposed and correctly *developed*. The negative matched the paper.

89

"U" and "O" Position Experiments

Summary

1. The "U" and "O" positions are indications of the range of modern films which numerically is 1 to 128.
2. *The Darkest Object Method* makes use of the "U" position set opposite the darkest object light value.
3. *The Brightest Object Method* uses the "O" position set opposite the brightest object light value.
4. Negative densities can be controlled through the use of the "U" and "O" positions.

Exposure Experiments

1. Choose a scene having a moderate range, 25 to 1, for example.
2. Measure close-up the darkest and brightest objects.
3. Make one exposure by setting the "U" position on the exposure meter dial opposite the darkest object light value.
4. Make another by setting the "O" position opposite the brightest object light value.
5. Develop and print. Note that, while one negative is thin and the other dense, both are correctly exposed and if printed correctly, both prints will be the same. Thus a number of correct exposures are possible for some scenes as long as the extreme light values fall on or between the "U" and "O" positions.

Film Ratings . . .

The Speed of Films

No exposure meter would be worth while if there were no accommodation made for adjusting it to various films and their varied speeds. There are approximately two to three hundred films on the market today. Their characteristics and speeds are duplicated among products of various manufacturers, but notwithstanding that fact there are a tremendous number of speed variations.

These different films are available to meet the varying needs of photographers. Here is a process film for copying, an ortho or a slow panchromatic emulsion for commercial purposes, a medium to high speed pan for portraiture and action pictures, and many other emulsions to meet many other needs. The exposure meter must be adaptable to all types, kinds and speeds of modern and future films. To do this, a speed system must be set up before the exposure meter can be considered to be complete.

There are many film speed systems which rate films. They include the German DIN system, the English H & D (named after Hurter & Driffield* who suggested and used it), the English, German and American Scheiner Systems and the arbitrary ratings assigned by film manufacturers. The only system which we will consider is the Weston speed system which was originated because the Weston engineer who designed the original photoelectric exposure meter was not satisfied with the accuracy of the available methods of rating film speeds. His

* Hurter and Driffield were two English scientists who put photography on a scientific basis. Their researches are the source from which all modern photography springs.

91

method has been found to be so accurate that the Weston speed of a film has become almost universally adopted in photography. Then too Weston meters are calibrated for this speed system, and the use of a Weston meter is the theme of this book.

As a matter of general interest, let us describe the steps taken in arriving at the Weston speed of a film.

First, film samples are obtained. All film is purchased from regular photographic dealers in various parts of the country. If the sample is of 35mm film, three pieces are obtained about 12 inches in length. Cut film is used in the 8x10 size and cut to 1x10 inches.

The second step is to expose three samples of each film on a machine known as a sensitometer. This sensitometer exposes portions of the film strip variably so that, when it is developed, it will form a step wedge, each step of which has been exposed to a definite measured quantity of light.

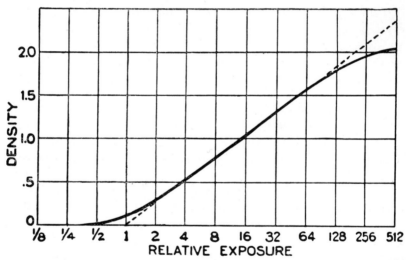

69. *A Typical H & D Curve.* Dotted extensions represent the slope of the gamma line.

Then each of the three samples is developed in a developing machine at a constant temperature with constant agitation, and each of the three for a different length of time. After a short-stop bath, careful fixing, washing and drying, three density strips are thus obtained.

The next move is to measure the density of each step of each strip. Since the exposure is known for each step, and the density is measurable on a densitometer, a curve can be plotted using the logarithm of the exposure on the horizontal axis and the measured density on the vertical axis. The curve resulting is known as the H & D Curve, named for Hurter and Driffield, who first invented and used it. From this curve, the Weston speed is calculated.

The accompanying typical H & D curve will be used to illustrate the way in which the Weston speed is calculated. First, the slope of the straight line portion of the curve is measured and the density corresponding to this value read off the vertical axis. Then the point on the curve corresponding to this density value is found and a line dropped to a point on the horizontal axis representing log exposure. The anti-logarithm of the point thus determined is found and the Weston speed is calculated through the use of the following formula:

$$W = \frac{e}{4}$$

Where:

$W =$ Weston speed.

$e =$ Exposure, the value of which has just been described.

$4 =$ Constant.

The tests are performed for three different developing times in the developer recommended by the film manufacturer. After as many as ten or twelve sets of three strips each have been exposed, developed, measured and analyzed, the results are averaged and a group film rating is assigned.

It is a fact that film speed ratings vary considerably with developing techniques. Furthermore, additional variations result from improperly adjusted and marked shutter speeds and apertures. For these reasons it has been found desirable to rate film speed in a group rating determined by controlled laboratory tests. The film can be used through the range of this group if the developing technique varies from the recommended procedure. For example, a film rated at a group number of 100 should be used at 100 if the manufacturer's recommended developing procedure is followed. For developers or developing times other than those recommended, the photographer can use speeds from 80 to 125 depending upon whether his technique results in a slower or faster rating.

Fine grain developers and high film speeds are at odds! If one uses a fine grain developer, *the film speed will be reduced.* A good general rule is to believe the meter rather than the developer manufacturer. It can be said most honestly and scientifically that there is no really fine grain developer which does not reduce the speed of film by *at least 50%.* This applies particularly to those developers which are put in fancy bottles, labeled in brilliant colors, advertised in glowing terms and sold for many times what they are worth. A safe rule is to reduce film ratings to at least 50% of the rated speed when using these developers.

70. Accuracy is maintained in all work of the Weston Sensitometric Laboratory.

Exposure Variations and Summary

Equipment Errors

Sometimes camera equipment is not as accurate as one might be led to believe. There is no reliable way to correct the errors occurring in photographic apparatus. Therefore incorrect exposure can result even if an accurate exposure meter is used. The simplest method of compensating for these errors is to change the speed ratings of the films you use. If your negatives are consistently underexposed, decrease the film rating. If overexposed consistently, increase it. Usually this will not be necessary, but if indicated, don't hesitate to do so.

The Weston system of rating films progresses arithmetically. That is, a film having a rating of 24 would be twice as fast as one rated at 12. A film rated at 8 would be one third as fast as the one at 24, while a film rated at 100 would have four times the speed of one rated at 24 Weston. Therefore if it is necessary to reduce the speed a certain percentage for a specific emulsion because of fine grain developers, or because of equipment errors, all other films should be reduced by the same percentage for that method of processing.

Summary

1. There are many systems of rating film speeds. The Weston system was designed specifically for the Weston exposure meters.
2. Developing techniques influence film speeds. If a fine grain developer is to be used, decrease the film speed by as much as 50% of the rated value.

And now, one last word about film speeds to explode some fanciful bubbles——. *There is no developer which can increase the film speed and still retain or attain fine grain.* This is based on laboratory research, scientific fact, and experimental proof.

71. Planned exposure combined with controlled development produced this attractive silhouette-type picture along the shores of Kezar Lake, Lovell, Maine. Photo by George French.

Film Development

THE making of a decent, printable negative consists of two parts—exposure and development. A correctly exposed film can be utterly ruined by being incorrectly developed. Hence correct development is a tremendously important part of the making of a good photograph. On the other hand, a correctly developed negative is worthless if the exposure is in error. Since we have already considered the way to expose the film correctly, the time has come to discuss development.

In general, exposure controls the density of the shadows and development controls the density of the highlights. Development also controls the relation of the densities of the shadows and the highlights to each other—in other words, the density range of the negative.

The density range is expressed by the numerical difference between the minimum density (the thinnest part, the shadow) and the maximum density (the densest part, the highlight). For example, the thinnest part of the negative might have a value of 0.3 expressed in density units, while the densest portion might have a value of 1.4. The density range would then be 1.4 minus 0.3 or 1.1.

In discussing the brightness range method of using the exposure meter, you will remember that by dividing the light value of the brightest object in the scene by the light value of the darkest object, a value for the *Scene Brightness Range* can be obtained. The Scene Brightness Range directly affects the *Negative Density Range*—the greater the scene range, the greater will be the negative density range.

The negative density range concerns the photographer because the density range that can be handled by photographic paper is limited. Each grade of paper of the commonly available four will handle a negative of a certain negative density range. To illustrate:

No. 1 paper will print correctly a negative having a range of 1.3.

No. 2 paper will handle a negative of a range, 1.0.

No. 3 paper with a range of .8.

No. 4 paper, a range of .65-.7.

It is, of course, necessary to keep negative density ranges within the scope of the available papers, for what is known as "print contrast" is nothing more than the relationship between the negative and paper ranges. A good photograph always retains detail in the darkest shadow and modelling in the brightest highlight. That means that the negative and paper *must fit* each other.

It will be noted that there are three ranges that concern the photographer:

1. The Scene Range.
2. The Negative Range.
3. The Paper Range.

All three of these ranges are interrelated and are dependent upon the paper range. It is perfectly logical that if the paper range is limited, it will limit the negative range which in turn depends upon the scene range.

Since development controls the negative density range, it can be varied for various scene ranges, and, if controlled carefully, the negative density range can always be the same irrespective of the scene. To more fully understand the manner in which development controls negative density range, it will be necessary to consider the term of "gamma."

Gamma is the term designating the slope of the straight line portion of the H & D curve. The slope of a curve, in non-mathematical language, is the inclination of the line in question. A road straight up a high mountain would be steeper, or would have a greater slope than one built straight up the side of a lower mountain. If you can visualize the straight line portion of the H & D curve as being the road up the mountain, you'll get the point. The greater the slope, the greater is its numerical value, and the lesser the slope, the less is its numerical value. And "gamma" is merely the expression applied to the numerical value of the slope.

It would seem logical that the greater the slope, the higher would be the maximum altitude of the mountain. Just so with the H & D curve; the greater the slope (the gamma) the greater will be the maximum density of the negative. The minimum density changes very little regardless of changes of gamma. Hence the higher the gamma, the greater will be the maximum density, and since the minimum density is subject to little variation, *the higher the gamma, the greater will be the density range of the negative.* And hence, the greater the contrast of the negative.

Gamma, or the numerical value of the slope of the H & D curve, is controlled by:

1. The time of development.
2. The temperature of the developer.
3. The characteristics of both film and developer.
4. Agitation during development.

Standardizing most of these variables—the kind of film and developer, the method of agitation during development and the temperature at which the development is carried out—leaves the factor of time controlling the gamma to which a negative is to be developed. The greater the time, the higher the gamma.

Now, let us consider each of these variables and see what can be done about them.

Usually nothing can be done about the scene brightness range but to measure it. To do this, close-up readings are taken with the exposure meter of the darkest and brightest objects in the scene. The brightest object value is then divided by the darkest object value and the numerical term for the scene range is arrived at. For example, the brightest object in the scene might have a light value of 600, and the darkest object, 50. The scene range is then $\frac{600}{50}$ or 12. If the darkest object had a value of 5 the scene range would then be 120 $\left(\frac{600}{5}\right)$.

The next variable to consider is paper range. Experience has shown that the best print will result if the negative just matches the density range of a No. 2 paper which is 1.0.

Use of Time — Gamma Tables

Since we cannot control the scene range, and the paper range is fixed at 1.0, the only thing possible is to vary the development to arrive at a negative density range of 1.0. In other words, we can vary the "gamma" of development so that the negative contrast range just meets the paper range.

For a practical procedure:

1. Measure the scene range as suggested.
2. Consult the accompanying curve which shows the relationship between gamma and scene brightness range to arrive at the negative range desired—1.0.
3. Consult a time-gamma table prepared for that developer and film, and choose the time necessary to attain the gamma necessary.
4. Develop for that time with the recommended agitation.

By aiming at a No. 2 paper, if an error is made somewhere along the line, a No. 1 or No. 3 paper can be used. But never will an unprintable negative result. For an unprintable negative is one where the negative density range exceeds or is less than any available paper range, and by using this method, even though a small error is made, a paper can be found easily to fit the negative.

Incidentally, time-gamma tables can be obtained from the manufacturer of the film you use. These tables are accurate providing the processing is carried out in the developer recommended by the manufacturer. There is no excuse for using a film developer other than that recommended; if there were a developer which would yield better results than the one he happened to put together, it is only logical that he would recom-

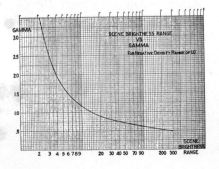

72. The relationship between scene brightness range and gamma can be seen in this curve.

mend it. For the film manufacturer is primarily concerned that you get good results with his film.

If you must use a different developer than that recommended, remember to investigate that developer's influence on film speed. Fine grain developers decrease film speeds, and a few maximum energy developers increase it, many times. They increase it because of higher gammas (often resulting in unprintable negatives) and they materially increase grain size. The time-gamma tables supplied by the manufacturer cannot, of course, be used with a different developer than that specified.

Many times, it is very difficult to control the temperature of the developer. To measure the temperature is a simple matter, but to control it is a different case. Because this control is so difficult, there are *time-gamma temperature curves* and tables available, and for them we refer you to the "Photo-Lab-Index"

73. Correct exposure and full development helped to give the crisp black and white effectiveness of this picture. George French made this rainbow shot at Lubec, Maine in bright sunlight, K-2 filter, 1/5 sec., at f/28, fast pan film.

Development Experiments

by Henry M. Lester, which contains upward of 250 film-developer combinations.

This system of development control is naturally applicable only to cut film or plates where each picture can be developed individually. Only serious photographers will be interested in this control, however, and they generally use cut film or plate cameras. However, the 35mm worker can also follow these suggestions by using short lengths of film and exposing each length to the one scene.

Summary

1. The printing quality of a negative is affected by:
   a. The scene range.
   b. The negative range.
   c. The paper range.
2. The scene range can be measured by an exposure meter of the Universal type, while the paper range is known.
3. The negative range is controlled by the gamma of the negative which can be varied by varying the development time.
4. All negatives can be matched to the available paper range by controlling the negative density range in accordance with the curve in this chapter.
5. Stick to the developers recommended by the film manufacturer and thereby take advantage of the development data he can supply.

Development Experiments

1. Choose a long range scene and make three identical exposures. Develop one the standard time to attain a gamma of .8, another half that time and the third twice the time.
2. Print all three on normal paper. Note that the normally and overdeveloped negatives will not yield good prints, while the underdeveloped one will.
3. Repeat for a flat scene. Here, the so-called "over-developed" negative will yield the best print.
4. Therefore it can be seen that developing times must be varied as the scene range varies.

The Theory of an Exposure

Meter • A Brightness Meter

THE exposure meter is fundamentally a brightness meter, an instrument so designed that it will measure the intensity of illumination reflected from a surface. To accomplish this, a baffle is placed in front of the sensitive surface of the photoelectric cell. This limits the light which can fall upon the cell surface to a definite angle on either side of the perpendicular. The total angle is known as the acceptance angle.

The acceptance angle, limited by the design of the baffle, in turn limits the area from which reflected light may reach the cell. The smaller the angle, the smaller the area when the meter is held a constant distance from the surface. The greater the angle, the greater the area. It is the fact of this limiting angle which changes an illumination meter to a brightness meter. And why a brightness meter? Because the camera makes pictures with brightness, with reflected light, and to measure the light which affects the film, it is only natural to measure brightness—with a brightness meter.

The Exposure Guide Dial

Various objects in the scene reflect various amounts of light —or have different brightnesses. The brighter the object, the denser will be its image on the negative. The greatest brightness in the scene will always yield the densest image and the smallest brightness, the thinnest. All other brightnesses will fall some place between the two extremes.

These brightnesses can all be measured; hence a definite value can be assigned to each one. Around the outside of the exposure guide dial on the Universal exposure meter are light values, each one matching some value in the scene. As we learned before, the "U" position indicates the darkest object that will be correctly exposed and the "O" position, the brightest. All other objects will fall some place between.

Since the H & D curve is merely a mathematical expression of negative density plotted against exposure, the exposure guide dial on the meter can be fitted to an average H & D curve. Each increasing light value on the curve will have a correspondingly increased density. Since the curve is reproduced on the dial in another form, each increasing light value will have a definite density, and the increment would be $.1x_\gamma$, where γ represents the degree of contrast to which the negative has been developed. If the gamma is 1.0, the increment of density increase will be 0.1 per brightness step. If the gamma is 0.8, the increment will be .08, and so forth.

The exposure meter will allow the photographer to achieve three kinds of exposure:

1. *Normal* exposure.
2. *Correct* exposure.
3. *Selective* exposure.

Normal exposure is one where the mid-brightness in the scene is located at the middle of the H & D curve and the brightest and darkest brightness are the same distance away from this midpoint. Normal exposure is the result of using the brightness range method.

Correct exposure results when all object brightness in the scene fall on some portion of the film range. For example, the darkest object may fall on the curve at the minimum point of separation, the brightest at the maximum point, or they may be any place on the curve as long as the two extremes both are on the usable portion of the curve. Practically all methods of using the meter will result in correct exposure as defined, with the possible exception of the close-up single reading method.

Selective exposure can be defined as one where the photographer exposes so that a specific object brightness falls on a selected point on the H & D curve. For example, using the close-up reading method and the normal arrow, the photographer selects an object to receive a specific exposure—the one in the middle of the curve.

104

The Inverse Square Law

Many photographers, knowing of the inverse square law of light, have wondered why it is possible to obtain correct exposure by taking close-up readings. They reason that since the intensity of light decreases as the object distance increases, a higher light value will be obtained close-up than if the meter were used at a greater distance. The reason that an exposure meter measures brightness correctly, regardless of its distance from such a surface, is the direct result of the inverse square law.

This can be understood from the following reasoning. If a Meter is held at a distance of 6 feet from a surface of uniform brightness, and by its acceptance angle covers an area of say 4 square feet, then at 3 feet it will cover an area of 1 square foot as a result of simple geometry. The effect on the exposure meter for each square foot of light surface at the six foot distance will be ¼ of that at 3 feet as a result of the inverse square law, but at 6 feet the meter is acted upon by 4 times the area of light than at 3 feet. The increased light area at the greater distance exactly compensates for the reduction produced by the increased distance, so that the effect upon the meter is the same for both.

Brightness meters are calibrated in light per unit area, and in the case of Weston Universal exposure meters, candles (*light*) per square foot (*area*).

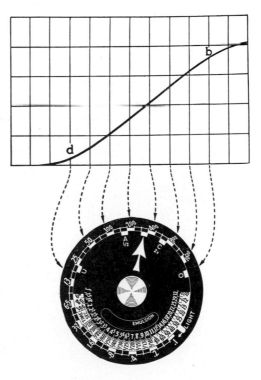

74. How the exposure guide dial fits the H & D curve.

Average Brightness Values

Light Integration

When an exposure meter is used at the position of the camera, it integrates or averages the light from all parts of the scene. If the area of the scene is composed of 50% having a light value of 500, 25% measuring 160, 10% measuring 300, and 15% measuring 25, the meter reading would be the sum of all in the percentage of their presence. In the above example:

$$50\% \ \text{of} \ 500 = 250$$
$$25\% \ \text{of} \ 160 = 40$$
$$10\% \ \text{of} \ 300 = 30$$
$$15\% \ \text{of} \ 25 = \frac{4}{324}$$

Therefore the brightness value for that scene would have an average value of 324 and the meter would indicate that value when used from the camera position. It will be seen immediately that if the scene is made up largely of one brightness with a small object having a materially different brightness, the chances are that the small object will be incorrectly exposed. Let us cite a definite example.

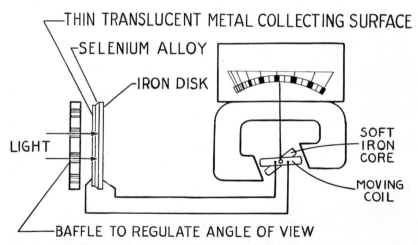

75. Diagram of the exposure meter. The cell is a miniature power plant whose output is measured by a microammeter.

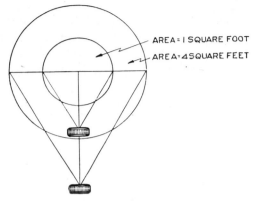

AREA = I SQUARE FOOT

AREA = 4 SQUARE FEET

76. The inverse square law is neutralized by the areas measured by the exposure meter. Therefore close-up readings can be made without error.

A scene is made up of one dark backlighted tree trunk surrounded by brightly illuminated white concrete. The trunk had a light value of 10 and made up 2% of the scene area. The concrete had a value of 1000 and made up 98% of the scene:

$$
\begin{array}{rl}
2\% \text{ of } 10 & = \quad .2 \\
98\% \text{ of } 1000 & = 980. \\
\hline
& 980.2
\end{array}
$$

Let us call this 1000 because of its nearness to 980.2. Set the normal arrow at 1000, and it will be seen that 10 is below the "U" position and therefore will necessarily be under-exposed. But by setting the arrow midway between 10 and 1000, both objects will lie within the scene range. Here then is the best argument for the two-reading brightness range method.

Theory of the Photoelectric Cell

There is considerably more known about the practical application of the cell, than about its theory. It is reasonably easy to explain what happens, but to carry out the theory and make a cell is something else again.

Without delving too deeply into physics and theoretical chemistry, let us see what happens. The cell is made of a form of the element selenium coated on an iron base. The light falling on its surface is a form of energy, and this energy in turn releases electrons from the selenium. These electrons collect on the surface of the selenium, and give it a negative electrical charge. The iron base of the cell will therefore be positive with respect to the coating. Hence, by the action of light, a miniature electrical power plant is set up, and by contacting both the front and rear surfaces, there is started a flow of electrons. A flow of electrons *is* an electric current, and being measurable, its quantity can be made known by means of an electrical measuring instrument. The action of light energy on the sensitive selenium surface is continuous and the number of electrons, or amount of electricity thus generated, is directly proportional to the amount of light.

Since the action of the cell is photoelectric nothing is used up and theoretically these cells can keep up their action forever. However, accidental damage can end their life.

Spectral Sensitivity of the Cell

White light is considered as being made up of all colors, and since light is the motivating energy of the photoelectric cell, it follows that individual colors of light will affect the cell. The cell is more sensitive to some colors than to others, just as are the human eye and the photographic film. Their response to lights of various colors, having the same energy rate is called their sensitivity. The curve (figure 77) shows the sensitivity of the eye, of the cell and of an average panchromatic emulsion.

It will be noticed that the cell is sensitive to more colors than the human eye, and that the film is more sensitive than the cell to longer wavelengths of light. Fortunately, the cell and film sensitivity are sufficiently close for practical purposes, the small difference being taken care of by the film speed rating. There is also a difference between the sensitivity of the cell and orthochromatic and color blind films. Here again the difference is taken care of by the film speed rating.

Both films and cell are affected by the color of the light source, but both are affected in the same way. That is, when the film is affected by a change in the color of the light source, so is the cell. If the light is such that a longer exposure than usual is needed, the light will affect the cell in the same manner, and the meter will indicate a longer exposure. However, the difference between sunlight and tungsten is too great for this automatic compensation, hence there are two listed speeds for each film, one for daylight and one for tungsten.

108

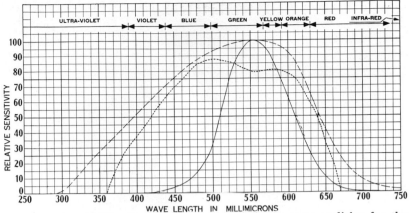

77. *Spectral Sensitivity Curves* showing the relative response to light: for the average photoelectric cell (long dashes), panchromatic film (short dash line), and the human eye (solid line).

There have been many comments written concerning the need of film rating compensation early in the morning and late in the afternoon. In truth the change in light quality is insufficient to make this necessary. The automatic compensation due to the closeness of the meter and film responses will handle the situation quite nicely.

109

78. Sgt. Doris Day, WAC, bravely exposed this picture for the foreground, upon which the camera was sharply focused. The vicious animal is being trained for a "warning dog" to warn his guards of proximity of prowlers. A soldier, just out of range of the camera, infuriates the animal by slapping at him. Official photograph, Mather Field, California.

110

Zero Setting of

Instrument Pointer

OCCASIONALLY an electrical instrument will wander off zero. The exposure meter, being fundamentally an electrical instrument, will occasionally indicate a light value or perhaps be below zero when no light reaches the cell. For that reason a zero corrector was placed on the instrument. It is wise to check occasionally the zero setting of the meter by holding the instrument at a 45° angle with the hand or a piece of cardboard covering the cell. If the instrument is off zero, merely turn the screw on the face of the meter until the pointer is on zero. This will not correct the reading if the instrument is damaged. A wander ing from zero which will occur occasionally and an incorrect reading resulting from damage are two distinct things.

Static Charge

Very infrequently the glass covering the scale of the exposure meter may carry a *static charge*. This would, of course, influence the pointer action since a static charge is an electrical charge and, as such, would influence an electrical instrument. If in cold weather (when this is most apt to happen), there is reasonable evidence to believe a static charge is influencing the meter, merely blow on the glass cover of the scale. This will remove the charge if one is present.

The Exposure Meter for Enlarging

There have been many suggestions concerning the use of the exposure meter for enlarging. Most of these are impractical and often more complicated and time-consuming than the usual test strip method of timing enlargements. The Eastman Kodak

Exposure for Enlarging

Company has issued directions on the use of a Model 715 or 650 Weston Universal exposure meter with the Eastman Precision Enlarger as follows:

An Exposure Meter bracket A which takes the Weston Exposure Meter, Model 715, is supplied as an accessory (the Model 650 Weston Meter can also be used by changing the clamps). The sliding plate of the bracket fastens into the lower bellows frame where the lens is normally positioned. When using this device the lens is put into the lens opening of the bracket. The meter is then put into a fixed position just below the enlarger lens position and the device is ready for use. It will be noted that the projection lens and the exposure meter are both mounted on a sliding bracket so that meter readings can be quickly made by simply interchanging lens and meter. It will be found that with this equipment it is an easy matter to print any roll of negatives in considerably less time than by the test strip method and produce a collection of prints which are all of better than average quality.

Assuming standard conditions of enlarger illumination and development, only three variables have to be considered in determining the proper exposure time for any negative at any magnification. These are: (1) Negative opacity, (2) Degree of enlargement, and (3) Paper emulsion speed. In order to maintain constant enlarger illumination the lens is operated at one aperture, say f/ 8 or f/ 11, at all times. The negative opacity is determined in each case by reflecting the light transmitted by the negative onto the photoelectric cell. The degree of enlargement is determined by measuring the distance between the projected images of the notches in the negative carrier. The paper emulsion speed is found by making one test print from any negative in the usual manner, noting the printing time.

To explain the procedure to be followed in using this device, the following example is given:

1. Assume that a miniature negative of average density is placed in the enlarger, focused, and a test print of acceptable quality made in the usual fashion.
2. Observe the magnification by measuring the distance between images of the negative carrier V notches. This distance in inches gives the magnification directly, since the

notches in the carrier are separated by one inch. Let us assume that in this case the magnification equals 8. (It will be found convenient to set the machine at some even magnification prior to making the test print).

3. The correct exposure time for this print is noted. Let us assume it to be ten seconds.

4. Without disturbing the focus of the machine the Weston meter is moved into the lens position with the hinged mirror set in the 45° position and a meter reading taken. Let us assume the meter reading to be 50. Now the fundamental assumption is made that the f-number scale on the Weston meter will be used as a magnification scale in printing. Therefore, 8 on the f-number scale is located opposite 10 on the time scale. Then, without disturbing the location of these two scales, depress button B and then turn tab I until the arrow is set opposite a light value of 50. From then on, tab I will be left undisturbed for all other negatives that print satisfactorily on the same grade of paper and from the same paper batch.

5. We are now in a position to determine the printing time for any negative at any magnification provided the same batch of paper is used. Let us assume that a second negative is selected for printing, placed in the machine, and focused at a magnification of 16.

6. This time the meter reading is found to be 100. (It should be observed that the meter reading is not taken until after the image is focused). Setting the arrow of the meter scale on the light value of 100 we find a printing of 20 seconds appears opposite the magnification of 16 (on the f-number scale). Naturally, this assumes that the batch of paper, developer, and developer temperature remain the same as in the test print.

Briefly, the correct printing time for any negative at any magnification is secured by setting the indicator arrow opposite the meter reading, and then reading the printing time directly opposite the magnification being used.

113

Incident Light Measurements

When working with the Weston 715 meter it will be found convenient to open the baffle for reading negatives of greater than average density. However, before doing this, a test print should be made with the baffle open to insure that both the high and low sensitivity scales agree in calibration.

To eliminate the necessity of recalibrating the paper speed when changing from one negative size to another, the reflecting mirror in the exposure meter bracket has been hinged along one edge. Tilting the mirror permits the operator to adjust the quantity of light incident upon the photocell surface. For example, when a larger negative is to be used the mirror is tilted until the meter reading is brought back to the value it formerly had for the smaller negative size. This adjustment is more easily made without a negative in the carrier, and the magnification is held constant during the change. (Since the lenses will be changed in going from one negative size to another, it will be necessary to refocus to the same magnification).

Measuring Incident Illumination

The exposure meter is, of course, an instrument to measure reflected light, or brightness. The Weston Universal meters (Models 617, 640 and 715) are calibrated in *candles per square foot*, a measure of brightness. These instruments can be used to measure incident illumination in *foot-candles* if desired. The following relationship exists between candles per square foot, and foot-candles:

$$\pi B = ER$$

where

$\quad$ B = Candles per square foot.
$\quad$ E = Foot-candles.
$\quad$ R = Reflection coefficient of surface being measured, and
$\quad$ π = constant (3.1416)

Hence, by taking a close-up reading of any surface, if the reflection coefficient is known, the incident illumination can be determined.

114

Care and Repair of Exposure Meter

It is known that white typing paper has a reflection coefficient of about .8. Hence, by taking a close-up reading of a pad of white typing paper (pad to eliminate the slight tendency toward transparency of a single sheet), substituting the reading in the above formula, the value for the incident illumination in foot-candles can be found. It will be found that:

$$E = \frac{\pi\ B}{R}$$
$$E = \frac{\pi\ B}{.8}$$
$$E = 4.\ \times\ B\ \text{(approximately)}$$

An excellent approximation can therefore be obtained by multiplying the close-up meter reading by four. The result—incident illumination in foot-candles.

Care of an Exposure Meter

Given reasonable care, the photographer can expect a long life from his meter. But the instrument is made in much the same manner as a fine watch and should be given equal consideration. One cannot drop his meter and expect it to work satisfactorily.

Rough handling will damage the electrical instrument portion of the meter. Excessive heat and moisture will harm the cell. By excessive heat is meant heat in excess of 130°F. *Do Not Keep The Meter In The Glove Compartment* of your car in the summertime. Temperatures as high as 200°F. have been measured in this location.

By excessive moisture is meant a complete wetting of the meter—Don't!

Repair

While exposure meters will last a long time, when damaged the instruments can be repaired upon returning them direct to the manufacturer, or through the local photographic dealer.

Checking Meters

Two different models of Weston meters, or two meters of different manufacture should not be checked against each other, except in the laboratory.

The Meter as a Densitometer

Differences in acceptance angle, calibration and tolerance of accuracy make this unreliable. Two meters of the same manufacture can be checked against each other by pointing the meters at an evenly illuminated flat surface which is large enough so that only that surface is viewed by the two instruments. If the meters agree to within plus or minus 1 block on the scale, they can be said to agree (1 block represents 1/3 f/ stop which is sufficiently accurate for ordinary work).

The exposure meter can be checked by pointing the instrument at surfaces reflecting light of known intensity. A rough check can be made by using the following data,—

	Candles per square foot:
Clear, blue North Sky—(10:30 AM to 2:30 PM)	320—400
Average hand in bright sunlight (11 AM to 1 PM)	400
Green summer grass in sunlight (11 AM to 1 PM)	160

(Values shown are for the Weston Universal meters)

The photographer could measure white, gray, and black cards under certain conditions when the meter was new. In the future the instrument could be roughly checked against them.

NOTE: An exposure meter very seldom reads too high. If the reading is higher than expected, usually the test is in error rather than the meter. If the meter reads consistently too low—then it has been damaged.

The Weston Meter as a Densitometer

THE Weston Master exposure meter can be used as a densitometer through the construction of a simple light box and a hinged arm on which the meter can be clamped. The photograph on page 119 is practically self-explanatory. The light source is a No. 1 photoflood and the box itself is constructed of pine and plywood with a small door in the bottom for replacing the lamp.

116

79. No guessing on exposure when Konrad Cramer took this picture of his dog,
"Hypo." Made on Arrow Pan Film, developed in Defender 777 to a gamma of .55.
Weston meter showed a reading of 3.2 in the darkest corner. Outside, sunlit
snow pushed the meter arrow over 1000. Such a tremendous brightness range is
beyond the film range. A compromise was made by under exposing some shadow
detail to get a printable negative, $\frac{1}{4}$ second at f/32. A slight printing in of the
door and window was resorted to when making the print.

Using the Densitometer

At the top of the box, directly under the spot viewed by the exposure meter cell, is a ¼ inch hole. Under this aperture is a wedge shaped piece of metal arranged and fixed so that it can be slid in and out. This wedge partially obstructs the hole and thus makes its size variable.

To use the densitometer, the exposure meter is clamped to the arm with the low scale in place (0-50). The arm is then lowered and the metal wedge adjusted so that the meter indicates full scale (50). The densitometer is then ready for density measurements. The negative to be measured is placed on top of the box so that the spot to be measured is directly over the aperture, the arm lowered and the meter reading noted. The following table converts meter readings to density values *providing the meter reads 50 when no negative is in place:*

Meter Reading	Density Value	Meter Reading	Density Value
50	0	2.5	1.3
40	.1	2	1.4
32	.2	1.6	1.5
25	.3	1.3	1.6
20	.4	1.0	1.7
16	.5	.8	1.8
13	.6	.65	1.9
10	.7	.5	2.0
8	.8	.4	2.1
6.5	.9	.32	2.2
5	1.0	.25	2.3
4	1.1	.2	2.4
3.2	1.2		

Using Exposure Meters with Pin-Hole Lens

THE principles of optics which determine the f-stops of a pinhole lens are the same as for regular glass lenses. That is, the f-stop number is the distance from the pin-hole to the film (focal distance) divided by the aperture diameter of the pin-hole.

80. The exposure meter can be used as a densitometer. This illustrates one method of doing so.

For example, the pin-hole might be .0156 inches in diameter and the focal distance 4 inches. Dividing the latter by the former, the f-stop number is easily found——f/256.

This f-stop is not found on the exposure meter, so the following relationship must be used:

f-stop	Exposure Relationship
f/ 32	1
f/ 45	2
f/ 64	4
f/ 90	8
f/ 128	16
f/ 180	32
f/ 256	64
f/ 360	128
f/ 512	256
f/ 720	512
f/ 1024	1024

It will be seen that an f-stop of f/256 requires 64 times the exposure as that at f/ 32. Therefore, after using the exposure meter in the regular manner and computing the exposure

119

at f/ 32, the shutter speed should be multiplied by 64. The shutter speed for an aperture of f/ 720 would be that at f/ 32 multiplied by the proper factor found in the table, 512, and so forth.

If the f-stop computed is one not found in the table, f/325 for example, use the next higher value for the multiplying factor (128 found opposite f/ 360).

The exposure meter can be used with a regular glass lens operating at f-stops smaller than f/32 in the same manner.

Kodacolor

MUCH of the information about Kodachrome also applies to Kodacolor. But since the latter process results in a positive print, naturally the range is much less. It is possible to obtain an image on Kodacolor through a wide variation in exposure, but for best color reproduction no variation is permissible.

A single close-up reading should be made of the one *color* of principal interest and importance. Then the meter should be set with this light value, disregarding all other objects in the scene.

When using Kodacolor, scenes on gray days, in the shade or backlighted pictures should be avoided. Otherwise the negatives, even correctly exposed, will probably not be worth printing.

INDEX

Index

122

Index

NEW *Completely Revised*
V-TH EDITION

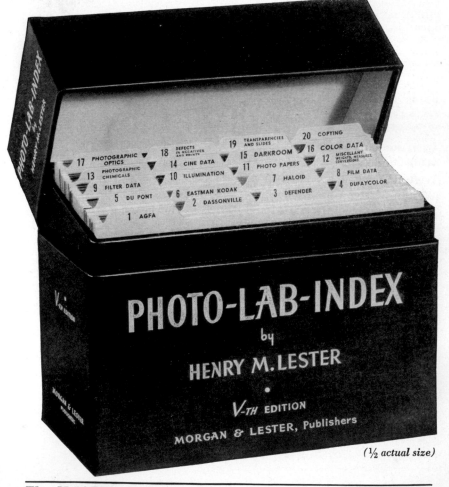

(½ *actual size*)

The MASTER Reference Work of Standard, Recommended